ANIMAL FARM

George Orwell

SPARK PUBLISHING

SPARKNOTES is a registered trademark of SparkNotes LLC

Spark Publishing
A Division of Barnes & Noble
120 Fifth Avenue
New York, NY 10011
www.sparknotes.com

ISBN-13: 978-1-4114-0514-1
ISBN-10: 1-4114-0514-5

Please submit changes or report errors to www.sparknotes.com/errors.

Printed in the United States.

10 9 8 7 6 5 4 3 2 1

CONTENTS

CONTEXT

EORGE ORWELL WAS THE PEN NAME of Eric Blair, a British political novelist and essayist whose pointed criticisms of political oppression propelled him into prominence toward the middle of the twentieth century. Born in 1903 to British colonists in Bengal, India, Orwell received his education at a series of private schools, including Eton, an elite school in England. His painful experiences with snobbishness and social elitism at Eton, as well as his intimate familiarity with the reality of British imperialism in India, made him deeply suspicious of the entrenched class system in English society. As a young man, Orwell became a socialist, speaking openly against the excesses of governments east and west and fighting briefly for the socialist cause during the Spanish Civil War, which lasted from 1936 to 1939.

Unlike many British socialists in the 1930s and 1940s, Orwell was not enamored of the Soviet Union and its policies, nor did he consider the Soviet Union a positive representation of the possibilities of socialist society. He could not turn a blind eye to the cruelties and hypocrisies of Soviet Communist Party, which had overturned the semifeudal system of the tsars only to replace it with the dictatorial reign of Joseph Stalin. Orwell became a sharp critic of both capitalism and communism, and is remembered chiefly as an advocate of freedom and a committed opponent of communist oppression. His two greatest anti-totalitarian novels—*Animal Farm* and *1984*—form the basis of his reputation. Orwell died in 1950, only a year after completing *1984,* which many consider his masterpiece.

A dystopian novel, *1984* attacks the idea of totalitarian communism (a political system in which one ruling party plans and controls the collective social action of a state) by painting a terrifying picture of a world in which personal freedom is nonexistent. *Animal Farm,* written in 1945, deals with similar themes but in a shorter and somewhat simpler format. A "fairy story" in the style of Aesop's fables, it uses animals on an English farm to tell the history of Soviet communism. Certain animals are based directly on Communist Party leaders: the pigs Napoleon and Snowball, for example, are figurations of Joseph Stalin and Leon Trotsky, respectively. Orwell uses the form of the fable for a number of aesthetic and political reasons. To better understand these, it is helpful to know at least the rudiments of Soviet history under Communist Party rule, beginning with the October Revolution of 1917.

In February 1917, Tsar Nicholas II, the monarch of Russia, abdicated and the socialist Alexander Kerensky became premier. At the end of October (November 7 on current calendars), Kerensky was ousted, and Vladimir Lenin, the architect of the Russian Revolution, became chief commissar. Almost immediately, as wars raged on virtually every Russian front, Lenin's chief allies began jockeying for power in the newly formed state; the most influential included Joseph Stalin, Leon Trotsky, Gregory Zinoviev, and Lev Kamenev. Trotsky and Stalin emerged as the most likely heirs to Lenin's vast power. Trotsky was a popular and charismatic leader, famous for his impassioned speeches, while the taciturn Stalin preferred to consolidate his power behind the scenes. After Lenin's death in 1924, Stalin orchestrated an alliance against Trotsky that included himself, Zinoviev, and Kaminev. In the following years, Stalin succeeded in becoming the unquestioned dictator of the Soviet Union and had Trotsky expelled first from Moscow, then from the Communist Party, and finally from Russia altogether in 1936. Trotsky fled to Mexico, where he was assassinated on Stalin's orders in 1940.

In 1934, Stalin's ally Serge Kirov was assassinated in Leningrad, prompting Stalin to commence his infamous purges of the Communist Party. Holding "show trials"—trials whose outcomes he and his allies had already decided—Stalin had his opponents officially denounced as participants in Trotskyist or anti-Stalinist conspiracies and therefore as "enemies of the people," an appellation that guaranteed their immediate execution. As the Soviet government's economic planning faltered and failed, Russia suffered under a surge of violence, fear, and starvation. Stalin used his former opponent as a tool to placate the wretched populace. Trotsky became a common national enemy and thus a source of negative unity. He was a frightening specter used to conjure horrifying eventualities, in comparison with which the current misery paled. Additionally, by associating his enemies with Trotsky's name, Stalin could ensure their immediate and automatic elimination from the Communist Party.

These and many other developments in Soviet history before 1945 have direct parallels in *Animal Farm*: Napoleon ousts Snowball from the farm and, after the windmill collapses, uses Snowball in his purges just as Stalin used Trotsky. Similarly, Napoleon becomes a dictator, while Snowball is never heard from again. Orwell was inspired to write *Animal Farm* in part by his experiences in a Trotskyist group during the Spanish Civil War, and Snowball certainly receives a more sympathetic portrayal than Napoleon. But though *Animal Farm* was written as an attack on a specific government, its general themes of oppression, suffering, and injustice have far broader application; modern readers have come to see Orwell's book as a powerful attack on any political, rhetorical, or military power that seeks to control human beings unjustly.

HISTORICAL CONTEXT

Russian society in the early twentieth century was bipolar: a tiny minority controlled most of the country's wealth, while the vast majority of the country's inhabitants were impoverished and oppressed peasants. Communism arose in Russia when the nation's workers and peasants, assisted by a class of concerned intellectuals known as the intelligentsia, rebelled against and overwhelmed the wealthy and powerful class of capitalists and aristocrats. They hoped to establish a socialist utopia based on the principles of the German economic and political philosopher Karl Marx.

In *Das Kapital (Capital)*, Marx advanced an economically deterministic interpretation of human history, arguing that society would naturally evolve—from a monarchy and aristocracy, to capitalism, and then on to communism, a system under which all property would be held in common. The dignity of the poor workers oppressed by capitalism would be restored, and all people would live as equals. Marx followed this sober and scholarly work with *The Communist Manifesto*, an impassioned call to action that urged, "Workers of the world, unite!"

In the Russia of 1917, it appeared that Marx's dreams were to become reality. After a politically complicated civil war, Tsar Nicholas II, the monarch of Russia, was forced to abdicate the throne that his family had held for three centuries. Vladimir Ilych Lenin, a Russian intellectual revolutionary, seized power in the name of the Communist Party. The new regime took land and industry from private control and put them under government supervision. This centralization of economic systems constituted the first steps in restoring Russia to the prosperity it had known before World War I and in modernizing the nation's primitive infrastructure, including bringing electricity to the countryside. After Lenin died in 1924, Joseph Stalin and Leon Trotsky jockeyed for control of the newly

Plot Overview

O LD MAJOR, A PRIZE-WINNING BOAR, gathers the animals of the Manor Farm for a meeting in the big barn. He tells them of a dream he has had in which all animals live together with no human beings to oppress or control them. He tells the animals that they must work toward such a paradise and teaches them a song called "Beasts of England," in which his dream vision is lyrically described. The animals greet Major's vision with great enthusiasm. When he dies only three nights after the meeting, three younger pigs—Snowball, Napoleon, and Squealer—formulate his main principles into a philosophy called Animalism. Late one night, the animals manage to defeat the farmer Mr. Jones in a battle, running him off the land. They rename the property Animal Farm and dedicate themselves to achieving Major's dream. The cart-horse Boxer devotes himself to the cause with particular zeal, committing his great strength to the prosperity of the farm and adopting as a personal maxim the affirmation "I will work harder."

At first, Animal Farm prospers. Snowball works at teaching the animals to read, and Napoleon takes a group of young puppies to educate them in the principles of Animalism. When Mr. Jones reappears to take back his farm, the animals defeat him again, in what comes to be known as the Battle of the Cowshed, and take the farmer's abandoned gun as a token of their victory. As time passes, however, Napoleon and Snowball increasingly quibble over the future of the farm, and they begin to struggle with each other for power and influence among the other animals. Snowball concocts a scheme to build an electricity-generating windmill, but Napoleon solidly opposes the plan. At the meeting to vote on whether to take up the project, Snowball gives a passionate speech. Although Napoleon gives only a brief retort, he then makes a strange noise, and nine attack dogs—the puppies that Napoleon had confiscated in order to "educate"—burst into the barn and chase Snowball from the farm. Napoleon assumes leadership of Animal Farm and declares that there will be no more meetings. From that point on, he asserts, the pigs alone will make all of the decisions—for the good of every animal.

Napoleon now quickly changes his mind about the windmill, and the animals, especially Boxer, devote their efforts to completing it.

One day, after a storm, the animals find the windmill toppled. The human farmers in the area declare smugly that the animals made the walls too thin, but Napoleon claims that Snowball returned to the farm to sabotage the windmill. He stages a great purge, during which various animals who have allegedly participated in Snowball's great conspiracy—meaning any animal who opposes Napoleon's uncontested leadership—meet instant death at the teeth of the attack dogs. With his leadership unquestioned (Boxer has taken up a second maxim, "Napoleon is always right"), Napoleon begins expanding his powers, rewriting history to make Snowball a villain. Napoleon also begins to act more and more like a human being—sleeping in a bed, drinking whisky, and engaging in trade with neighboring farmers. The original Animalist principles strictly forbade such activities, but Squealer, Napoleon's propagandist, justifies every action to the other animals, convincing them that Napoleon is a great leader and is making things better for everyone—despite the fact that the common animals are cold, hungry, and overworked.

Mr. Frederick, a neighboring farmer, cheats Napoleon in the purchase of some timber and then attacks the farm and dynamites the windmill, which had been rebuilt at great expense. After the demolition of the windmill, a pitched battle ensues, during which Boxer receives major wounds. The animals rout the farmers, but Boxer's injuries weaken him. When he later falls while working on the windmill, he senses that his time has nearly come. One day, Boxer is nowhere to be found. According to Squealer, Boxer has died in peace after having been taken to the hospital, praising the Rebellion with his last breath. In actuality, Napoleon has sold his most loyal and long-suffering worker to a glue maker in order to get money for whisky.

Years pass on Animal Farm, and the pigs become more and more like human beings—walking upright, carrying whips, and wearing clothes. Eventually, the seven principles of Animalism, known as the Seven Commandments and inscribed on the side of the barn, become reduced to a single principle reading "all animals are equal, but some animals are more equal than others." Napoleon entertains a human farmer named Mr. Pilkington at a dinner and declares his intent to ally himself with the human farmers against the laboring classes of both the human and animal communities. He also changes the name of Animal Farm back to the Manor Farm, claiming that this title is the "correct" one. Looking in at the party of elites through the farmhouse window, the common animals can no longer tell which are the pigs and which are the human beings.

CHARACTER LIST

Napoleon   The pig who emerges as the leader of Animal Farm after the Rebellion. Based on Joseph Stalin, Napoleon uses military force (his nine loyal attack dogs) to intimidate the other animals and consolidate his power. In his supreme craftiness, Napoleon proves more treacherous than his counterpart, Snowball.

Snowball   The pig who challenges Napoleon for control of Animal Farm after the Rebellion. Based on Leon Trotsky, Snowball is intelligent, passionate, eloquent, and less subtle and devious than his counterpart, Napoleon. Snowball seems to win the loyalty of the other animals and cement his power.

Boxer   The cart-horse whose incredible strength, dedication, and loyalty play a key role in the early prosperity of Animal Farm and the later completion of the windmill. Quick to help but rather slow-witted, Boxer shows much devotion to Animal Farm's ideals but little ability to think about them independently. He naïvely trusts the pigs to make all his decisions for him. His two mottoes are "I will work harder" and "Napoleon is always right."

Squealer   The pig who spreads Napoleon's propaganda among the other animals. Squealer justifies the pigs' monopolization of resources and spreads false statistics pointing to the farm's success. Orwell uses Squealer to explore the ways in which those in power often use rhetoric and language to twist the truth and gain and maintain social and political control.

Old Major   The prize-winning boar whose vision of a socialist utopia serves as the inspiration for the Rebellion. Three days after describing the vision and teaching the animals the song "Beasts of England," Major dies, leaving Snowball and Napoleon to struggle for control of his legacy. Orwell based Major on both the German political economist Karl Marx and the Russian revolutionary leader Vladimir Ilych Lenin.

Clover   A good-hearted female cart-horse and Boxer's close friend. Clover often suspects the pigs of violating one or another of the Seven Commandments, but she repeatedly blames herself for misremembering the commandments.

Moses   The tame raven who spreads stories of Sugarcandy Mountain, the paradise to which animals supposedly go when they die. Moses plays only a small role in *Animal Farm,* but Orwell uses him to explore how communism exploits religion as something with which to pacify the oppressed.

Mollie   The vain, flighty mare who pulls Mr. Jones's carriage. Mollie craves the attention of human beings and loves being groomed and pampered. She has a difficult time with her new life on Animal Farm, as she misses wearing ribbons in her mane and eating sugar cubes. She represents the petit bourgeoisie that fled from Russia a few years after the Russian Revolution.

Benjamin   The long-lived donkey who refuses to feel inspired by the Rebellion. Benjamin firmly believes that life will remain unpleasant no matter who is in charge. Of all of the animals on the farm, he alone comprehends the changes that take place, but he seems either unwilling or unable to oppose the pigs.

Muriel   The white goat who reads the Seven Commandments to Clover whenever Clover suspects the pigs of violating their prohibitions.

Mr. Jones   The often drunk farmer who runs the Manor Farm before the animals stage their Rebellion and establish Animal Farm. Mr. Jones is an unkind master who indulges himself while his animals lack food; he thus represents Tsar Nicholas II, whom the Russian Revolution ousted.

Mr. Frederick   The tough, shrewd operator of Pinchfield, a neighboring farm. Based on Adolf Hitler, the ruler of Nazi Germany in the 1930s and 1940s, Mr. Frederick proves an untrustworthy neighbor.

Mr. Pilkington   The easygoing gentleman farmer who runs Foxwood, a neighboring farm. Mr. Frederick's bitter enemy, Mr. Pilkington represents the capitalist governments of England and the United States.

Mr. Whymper   The human solicitor whom Napoleon hires to represent Animal Farm in human society. Mr. Whymper's entry into the Animal Farm community initiates contact between Animal Farm and human society, alarming the common animals.

Jessie and Bluebell   Two dogs, each of whom gives birth early in the novel. Napoleon takes the puppies in order to "educate" them.

Minimus   The poet pig who writes verse about Napoleon and pens the banal patriotic song "Animal Farm, Animal Farm" to replace the earlier idealistic hymn "Beasts of England," which Old Major passes on to the others.

Analysis of Major Characters

Napoleon

From the very beginning of the novella, Napoleon emerges as an utterly corrupt opportunist. Though always present at the early meetings of the new state, Napoleon never makes a single contribution to the revolution—not to the formulation of its ideology, not to the bloody struggle that it necessitates, not to the new society's initial attempts to establish itself. He never shows interest in the strength of Animal Farm itself, only in the strength of his power over it. Thus, the only project he undertakes with enthusiasm is the training of a litter of puppies. He doesn't educate them for their own good or for the good of all, however, but rather for his own good: they become his own private army or secret police, a violent means by which he imposes his will on others.

Although he is most directly modeled on the Soviet dictator Joseph Stalin, Napoleon represents, in a more general sense, the political tyrants that have emerged throughout human history and with particular frequency during the twentieth century. His namesake is not any communist leader but the early-eighteenth-century French general Napoleon, who betrayed the democratic principles on which he rode to power, arguably becoming as great a despot as the aristocrats whom he supplanted. It is a testament to Orwell's acute political intelligence and to the universality of his fable that Napoleon can easily stand for any of the great dictators and political schemers in world history, even those who arose after *Animal Farm* was written. In the behavior of Napoleon and his henchmen, one can detect the lying and bullying tactics of totalitarian leaders such as Josip Tito, Mao Tse-tung, Pol Pot, Augusto Pinochet, and Slobodan Milosevic treated in sharply critical terms.

SNOWBALL

Orwell's stint in a Trotskyist battalion in the Spanish Civil War—during which he first began plans for a critique of totalitarian communism—influenced his relatively positive portrayal of Snowball. As a parallel for Leon Trotsky, Snowball emerges as a fervent ideologue who throws himself heart and soul into the attempt to spread Animalism worldwide and to improve Animal Farm's infrastructure. His idealism, however, leads to his downfall. Relying only on the force of his own logic and rhetorical skill to gain his influence, he proves no match for Napoleon's show of brute force.

Although Orwell depicts Snowball in a relatively appealing light, he refrains from idealizing his character, making sure to endow him with certain moral flaws. For example, Snowball basically accepts the superiority of the pigs over the rest of the animals. Moreover, his fervent, single-minded enthusiasm for grand projects such as the windmill might have erupted into full-blown megalomaniac despotism had he not been chased from Animal Farm. Indeed, Orwell suggests that we cannot eliminate government corruption by electing principled individuals to roles of power; he reminds us throughout the novella that it is power itself that corrupts.

BOXER

The most sympathetically drawn character in the novel, Boxer epitomizes all of the best qualities of the exploited working classes: dedication, loyalty, and a huge capacity for labor. He also, however, suffers from what Orwell saw as the working class's major weaknesses: a naïve trust in the good intentions of the intelligentsia and an inability to recognize even the most blatant forms of political corruption. Exploited by the pigs as much or more than he had been by Mr. Jones, Boxer represents all of the invisible labor that undergirds the political drama being carried out by the elites. Boxer's pitiful death at a glue factory dramatically illustrates the extent of the pigs' betrayal. It may also, however, speak to the specific significance of Boxer himself: before being carted off, he serves as the force that holds Animal Farm together.

SQUEALER

Throughout his career, Orwell explored how politicians manipulate language in an age of mass media. In *Animal Farm,* the silver-tongued pig Squealer abuses language to justify Napoleon's actions and policies to the proletariat by whatever means seem necessary. By radically simplifying language—as when he teaches the sheep to bleat "Four legs good, two legs better!"—he limits the terms of debate. By complicating language unnecessarily, he confuses and intimidates the uneducated, as when he explains that pigs, who are the "brainworkers" of the farm, consume milk and apples not for pleasure, but for the good of their comrades. In this latter strategy, he also employs jargon ("tactics, tactics") as well as a baffling vocabulary of false and impenetrable statistics, engendering in the other animals both self-doubt and a sense of hopelessness about ever accessing the truth without the pigs' mediation. Squealer's lack of conscience and unwavering loyalty to his leader, alongside his rhetorical skills, make him the perfect propagandist for any tyranny. Squealer's name also fits him well: squealing, of course, refers to a pig's typical form of vocalization, and Squealer's speech defines him. At the same time, to squeal also means to betray, aptly evoking Squealer's behavior with regard to his fellow animals.

OLD MAJOR

As a democratic socialist, Orwell had a great deal of respect for Karl Marx, the German political economist, and even for Vladimir Ilych Lenin, the Russian revolutionary leader. His critique of Animal Farm has little to do with the Marxist ideology underlying the Rebellion but rather with the perversion of that ideology by later leaders. Major, who represents both Marx and Lenin, serves as the source of the ideals that the animals continue to uphold even after their pig leaders have betrayed them.

Though his portrayal of Old Major is largely positive, Orwell does include a few small ironies that allow the reader to question the venerable pig's motives. For instance, in the midst of his long litany of complaints about how the animals have been treated by human beings, Old Major is forced to concede that his own life has been long, full, and free from the terrors he has vividly sketched for his rapt audience. He seems to have claimed a false brotherhood with the other animals in order to garner their support for his vision.

THEMES, MOTIFS & SYMBOLS

THEMES

Themes are the fundamental and often universal ideas explored in a literary work.

THE CORRUPTION OF SOCIALIST IDEALS IN THE SOVIET UNION

Animal Farm is most famous in the West as a stinging critique of the history and rhetoric of the Russian Revolution. Retelling the story of the emergence and development of Soviet communism in the form of an animal fable, *Animal Farm* allegorizes the rise to power of the dictator Joseph Stalin. In the novella, the overthrow of the human oppressor Mr. Jones by a democratic coalition of animals quickly gives way to the consolidation of power among the pigs. Much like the Soviet intelligentsia, the pigs establish themselves as the ruling class in the new society.

The struggle for preeminence between Leon Trotsky and Stalin emerges in the rivalry between the pigs Snowball and Napoleon. In both the historical and fictional cases, the idealistic but politically less powerful figure (Trotsky and Snowball) is expelled from the revolutionary state by the malicious and violent usurper of power (Stalin and Napoleon). The purges and show trials with which Stalin eliminated his enemies and solidified his political base find expression in *Animal Farm* as the false confessions and executions of animals whom Napoleon distrusts following the collapse of the windmill. Stalin's tyrannical rule and eventual abandonment of the founding principles of the Russian Revolution are represented by the pigs' turn to violent government and the adoption of human traits and behaviors, the trappings of their original oppressors.

Although Orwell believed strongly in socialist ideals, he felt that the Soviet Union realized these ideals in a terribly perverse form. His novella creates its most powerful ironies in the moments in which Orwell depicts the corruption of Animalist ideals by those in power. For *Animal Farm* serves not so much to condemn tyranny or despotism as to indict the horrifying hypocrisy of tyrannies that base

themselves on, and owe their initial power to, ideologies of libera-
tion and equality. The gradual disintegration and perversion of the
Seven Commandments illustrates this hypocrisy with vivid force,
as do Squealer's elaborate philosophical justifications for the pigs'
blatantly unprincipled actions. Thus, the novella critiques the violence of the Stalinist regime against the human beings it ruled, and
also points to Soviet communism's violence against human logic,
language, and ideals.

THE SOCIETAL TENDENCY TOWARD CLASS STRATIFICATION

Animal Farm offers commentary on the development of class tyranny
and the human tendency to maintain and reestablish class structures
even in societies that allegedly stand for total equality. The novella
illustrates how classes that are initially unified in the face of a common enemy, as the animals are against the humans, may become
internally divided when that enemy is eliminated. The expulsion of
Mr. Jones creates a power vacuum, and it is only so long before the
next oppressor assumes totalitarian control. The natural division
between intellectual and physical labor quickly comes to express
itself as a new set of class divisions, with the "brainworkers" (as
the pigs claim to be) using their superior intelligence to manipulate
society to their own benefit. Orwell never clarifies in *Animal Farm*
whether this negative state of affairs constitutes an inherent aspect
of society or merely an outcome contingent on the integrity of a
society's intelligentsia. In either case, the novella points to the force
of this tendency toward class stratification in many communities
and the threat that it poses to democracy and freedom.

THE DANGER OF A NAÏVE WORKING CLASS

One of the novella's most impressive accomplishments is its portrayal not just of the figures in power but also of the oppressed
people themselves. *Animal Farm* is not told from the perspective of
any particular character, though occasionally it does slip into Clover's consciousness. Rather, the story is told from the perspective of
the common animals as a whole. Gullible, loyal, and hardworking,
these animals give Orwell a chance to sketch how situations of oppression arise not only from the motives and tactics of the oppressors
but also from the naïveté of the oppressed, who are not necessarily
in a position to be better educated or informed. When presented
with a dilemma, Boxer prefers not to puzzle out the implications of
various possible actions but instead to repeat to himself, "Napoleon
is always right." *Animal Farm* demonstrates how the inability or

unwillingness to question authority condemns the working class to suffer the full extent of the ruling class's oppression.

The Abuse of Language as Instrumental to the Abuse of Power

One of Orwell's central concerns, both in *Animal Farm* and in *1984*, is the way in which language can be manipulated as an instrument of control. In *Animal Farm*, the pigs gradually twist and distort a rhetoric of socialist revolution to justify their behavior and to keep the other animals in the dark. The animals heartily embrace Major's visionary ideal of socialism, but after Major dies, the pigs gradually twist the meaning of his words. As a result, the other animals seem unable to oppose the pigs without also opposing the ideals of the Rebellion. By the end of the novella, after Squealer's repeated reconfigurations of the Seven Commandments in order to decriminalize the pigs' treacheries, the main principle of the farm can be openly stated as "all animals are equal, but some animals are more equal than others." This outrageous abuse of the word "equal" and of the ideal of equality in general typifies the pigs' method, which becomes increasingly audacious as the novel progresses. Orwell's sophisticated exposure of this abuse of language remains one of the most compelling and enduring features of *Animal Farm*, worthy of close study even after we have decoded its allegorical characters and events.

Motifs

Motifs are recurring structures, contrasts, and literary devices that can help to develop and inform the text's major themes.

Songs

Animal Farm is filled with songs, poems, and slogans, including Major's stirring "Beasts of England," Minimus's ode to Napoleon, the sheep's chants, and Minimus's revised anthem, "Animal Farm, Animal Farm." All of these songs serve as propaganda, one of the major conduits of social control. By making the working-class animals speak the same words at the same time, the pigs evoke an atmosphere of grandeur and nobility associated with the recited text's subject matter. The songs also erode the animals' sense of individuality and keep them focused on the tasks by which they will purportedly achieve freedom.

STATE RITUAL

As Animal Farm shifts gears from its early revolutionary fervor to a phase of consolidation of power in the hands of the few, national rituals become an ever more common part of the farm's social life. Military awards, large parades, and new songs all proliferate as the state attempts to reinforce the loyalty of the animals. The increasing frequency of the rituals bespeaks the extent to which the working class in the novella becomes ever more reliant on the ruling class to define their group identity and values.

SYMBOLS

Symbols are objects, characters, figures, and colors used to represent abstract ideas or concepts.

ANIMAL FARM

Animal Farm, known at the beginning and the end of the novel as the Manor Farm, symbolizes Russia and the Soviet Union under Communist Party rule. But more generally, Animal Farm stands for any human society, be it capitalist, socialist, fascist, or communist. It possesses the internal structure of a nation, with a government (the pigs), a police force or army (the dogs), a working class (the other animals), and state holidays and rituals. Its location amid a number of hostile neighboring farms supports its symbolism as a political entity with diplomatic concerns.

THE BARN

The barn at Animal Farm, on whose outside walls the pigs paint the Seven Commandments and, later, their revisions, represents the collective memory of a modern nation. The many scenes in which the ruling-class pigs alter the principles of Animalism and in which the working-class animals puzzle over but accept these changes represent the way an institution in power can revise a community's concept of history to bolster its control. If the working class believes history to lie on the side of their oppressors, they are less likely to question oppressive practices. Moreover, the oppressors, by revising their nation's conception of its origins and development, gain control of the nation's very identity, and the oppressed soon come to depend upon the authorities for their communal sense of self.

The Windmill

The great windmill symbolizes the pigs' manipulation of the other animals for their own gain. Despite the immediacy of the need for food and warmth, the pigs exploit Boxer and the other common animals by making them undertake backbreaking labor to build the windmill, which will ultimately earn the pigs more money and thus increase their power. The pigs' declaration that Snowball is responsible for the windmill's first collapse constitutes psychological manipulation, as it prevents the common animals from doubting the pigs' abilities and unites them against a supposed enemy. The ultimate conversion of the windmill to commercial use is one more sign of the pigs' betrayal of their fellow animals. From an allegorical point of view, the windmill represents the enormous modernization projects undertaken in Soviet Russia after the Russian Revolution.

Summary & Analysis

Chapter I

Summary

As the novella opens, Mr. Jones, the proprietor and overseer of the Manor Farm, has just stumbled drunkenly to bed after forgetting to secure his farm buildings properly. As soon as his bedroom light goes out, all of the farm animals except Moses, Mr. Jones's tame raven, convene in the big barn to hear a speech by Old Major, a prize boar and pillar of the animal community. Sensing that his long life is about to come to an end, Major wishes to impart to the rest of the farm animals a distillation of the wisdom that he has acquired during his lifetime.

As the animals listen raptly, Old Major delivers up the fruits of his years of quiet contemplation in his stall. The plain truth, he says, is that the lives of his fellow animals are "miserable, laborious, and short." Animals are born into the world as slaves, worked incessantly from the time they can walk, fed only enough to keep breath in their bodies, and then slaughtered mercilessly when they are no longer useful. He notes that the land upon which the animals live possesses enough resources to support many times the present population in luxury; there is no natural reason for the animals' poverty and misery. Major blames the animals' suffering solely on their human oppressors. Mr. Jones and his ilk have been exploiting animals for ages, Major says, taking all of the products of their labor—eggs, milk, dung, foals—for themselves and producing nothing of value to offer the animals in return.

Old Major relates a dream that he had the previous night, of a world in which animals live without the tyranny of men: they are free, happy, well fed, and treated with dignity. He urges the animals to do everything they can to make this dream a reality and exhorts them to overthrow the humans who purport to own them. The animals can succeed in their rebellion only if they first achieve a complete solidarity or "perfect comradeship" of all of the animals against the humans, and if they resist the false notion spread by humans that animals and humans share common interests. A brief conversation arises in which the animals debate the status of rats as comrades. Major then provides a precept that will allow the animals to determine who their comrades are: creatures that walk on two legs are enemies; those with four legs or with wings are allies. He reminds his audience that the ways of man are completely corrupt: once the humans have been defeated, the animals must never adopt any of their habits; they must not live in a house, sleep in a bed, wear clothes, drink alcohol, smoke tobacco, touch money, engage in trade, or tyrannize another animal. He teaches the animals a song called "Beasts of England," which paints a dramatic picture of the utopian, or ideal, animal community of Major's dream. The animals sing several inspired choruses of "Beasts of England" with one voice—until Mr. Jones, thinking that the commotion bespeaks the entry of a fox into the yard, fires a shot into the side of the barn. The animals go to sleep, and the Manor Farm again sinks into quietude.

ANALYSIS

Although Orwell aims his satire at totalitarianism in all of its guises—communist, fascist, and capitalist—*Animal Farm* owes its structure largely to the events of the Russian Revolution as they unfolded between 1917 and 1944, when Orwell was writing the novella. Much of what happens in the novella symbolically parallels specific developments in the history of Russian communism, and several of the animal characters are based on either real participants in the Russian Revolution or amalgamations thereof. Due to the universal relevance of the novella's themes, we don't need to possess an encyclopedic knowledge of Marxist Leninism or Russian history in order to appreciate Orwell's satire of them. An acquaintance with certain facts from Russia's past, however, can help us recognize the particularly biting quality of Orwell's criticism (see Historical Background).

Because of *Animal Farm*'s parallels with the Russian Revolution, many readers have assumed that the novella's central importance lies in its exposure and critique of a particular political philosophy and practice, Stalinism. In fact, however, Orwell intended to critique Stalinism as merely one instance of the broader social phenomenon of totalitarianism, which he saw at work throughout the world: in fascist Germany (under Adolf Hitler) and Spain (under Francisco Franco), in capitalist America, and in his native England, as well as in the Soviet Union. The broader applicability of the story manifests itself in details such as the plot's setting—England.

Other details refer to political movements in other countries as well. The animals' song "Beasts of England," for example, parodies the "Internationale," the communist anthem written by the Paris Commune of 1871.

In order to lift his story out of the particularities of its Russian model and give it the universality befitting the importance of its message, Orwell turned to the two ancient and overlapping traditions of political fable and animal fable. Writers including Aesop (*Fables*), Jonathan Swift (especially in the Houyhnhnm section of *Gulliver's Travels*), Bernard Mandeville (*The Fable of the Bees*), and Jean de La Fontaine (*Fables*) have long cloaked their analyses of contemporary society in such parables in order to portray the ills of society in more effective ways. Because of their indirect approach, fables have a strong tradition in societies that censor openly critical works: the writers of fables could often claim that their works were mere fantasies and thus attract audiences that they might not have reached otherwise. Moreover, by setting human problems in the animal kingdom, a writer can achieve the distance necessary to see the absurdity in much of human behavior—he or she can abstract a human situation into a clearly interpretable tale. By treating the development of totalitarian communism as a story taking place on a small scale, reducing the vast and complex history of the Russian Revolution to a short work describing talking animals on a single farm, Orwell is able to portray his subject in extremely simple symbolic terms, presenting the moral lessons of the story with maximum clarity, objectivity, concision, and force.

Old Major's dream presents the animals with a vision of utopia, an ideal world. The "golden future time" that the song "Beasts of England" prophesies is one in which animals will no longer be subject to man's cruel domination and will finally be able to enjoy the fruits of their labors. The optimism of such lyrics as "Tyrant Man shall be o'erthrown" and "Riches more than mind can picture" galvanizes the animals' agitation, but unwavering belief in this lofty rhetoric, as soon becomes clear, prevents the common animals from realizing the gap between reality and their envisioned utopia.

CHAPTER II

Beasts of England, beasts of Ireland,
Beasts of every land and clime,
Hearken to my joyful tiding
Of the golden future time.

(See QUOTATIONS, *p. 52)*

SUMMARY
Three nights later, Old Major dies in his sleep, and for three months
the animals make secret preparations to carry out the old pig's dying wish of wresting control of the farm from Mr. Jones. The work
of teaching and organizing falls to the pigs, the cleverest of the animals, and especially to two pigs named Napoleon and Snowball.
Together with a silver-tongued pig named Squealer, they formulate
the principles of a philosophy called Animalism, the fundamentals
of which they spread among the other animals. The animals call
one another "Comrade" and take their quandaries to the pigs, who
answer their questions about the impending Rebellion. At first,
many of the animals find the principles of Animalism difficult to
understand; they have grown up believing that Mr. Jones is their
proper master. Mollie, a vain carriage horse, expresses particular
concern over whether she will be able to continue to enjoy the little
luxuries like eating sugar and wearing ribbons in the new utopia.
Snowball sternly reminds her that ribbons symbolize slavery and
that, in the animals' utopia, they would have to be abolished. Mollie halfheartedly agrees.

The pigs' most troublesome opponent proves to be Moses, the
raven, who flies about spreading tales of a place called Sugarcandy
Mountain, where animals go when they die—a place of great pleasure and plenty, where sugar grows on the hedges. Even though
many of the animals despise the talkative and idle Moses, they nevertheless find great appeal in the idea of Sugarcandy Mountain. The
pigs work very hard to convince the other animals of the falsehood
of Moses's teachings. Thanks to the help of the slow-witted but
loyal cart-horses, Boxer and Clover, the pigs eventually manage to
prime the animals for revolution.

The Rebellion occurs much earlier than anyone expected and
comes off with shocking ease. Mr. Jones has been driven to drink
after losing money in a lawsuit, and he has let his men become lazy,
dishonest, and neglectful. One day, Mr. Jones goes on a drinking

binge and forgets to feed the animals. Unable to bear their hunger, the cows break into the store shed and the animals begin to eat. Mr. Jones and his men discover the transgression and begin to whip the cows. Spurred to anger, the animals turn on the men, attack them, and easily chase them from the farm. Astonished by their success, the animals hurry to destroy the last remaining evidence of their subservience: chains, bits, halters, whips, and other implements stored in the farm buildings. After obliterating all signs of Mr. Jones, the animals enjoy a double ration of corn and sing "Beasts of England" seven times through, until it is time to sleep. In the morning, they admire the farm from a high knoll before exploring the farmhouse, where they stare in stunned silence at the unbelievable luxuries within. Mollie tries to stay inside, where she can help herself to ribbons and gaze at herself in the mirror, but the rest of the animals reprimand her sharply for her foolishness. The group agrees to preserve the farmhouse as a museum, with the stipulation that no animal may ever live in it.

The pigs reveal to the other animals that they have taught themselves how to read, and Snowball replaces the inscription "Manor Farm" on the front gate with the words "Animal Farm." Snowball and Napoleon, having reduced the principles of Animalism to seven key commandments, paint these commandments on the side of the big barn. The animals go to gather the harvest, but the cows, who haven't been milked in some time, begin lowing loudly. The pigs milk them, and the animals eye the five pails of milk desirously. Napoleon tells them not to worry about the milk; he says that it will be "attended to." Snowball leads the animals to the fields to begin harvesting. Napoleon lags behind, and when the animals return that evening, the milk has disappeared.

ANALYSIS

By the end of the second chapter, the precise parallels between the Russian Revolution and the plot of *Animal Farm* have emerged more clearly. The Manor Farm represents Russia under the part-feudal, part-capitalist system of the tsars, with Mr. Jones standing in for the moping and negligent Tsar Nicholas II. Old Major serves both as Karl Marx, who first espoused the political philosophy behind communism, and as Vladimir Lenin, who effected this philosophy's revolutionary expression. His speech to the other animals bears many similarities to Marx's Communist Manifesto and to Lenin's later writings in the same vein. The animals of the Manor Farm represent the workers and peasants of Russia, in whose name the Russian Revolution's leaders first struggled. Boxer and Clover, in particular, embody the aspects of the working class that facilitate the participation of the working class in revolution: their capacity for hard work, loyalty to each other, and lack of clear philosophical direction opens them up to the more educated classes' manipulation.

The pigs play the role of the intelligentsia, who organized and controlled the Russian Revolution. Squealer creates propaganda similar to that spread by revolutionaries via official organs such as the Communist Party newspaper *Pravda*. Moses embodies the Russian Orthodox Church, weakening the peasants' sense of revolutionary outrage by promising a utopia in the afterlife; the beer-soaked bread that Mr. Jones feeds him represents the bribes with which the Romanov dynasty (in which Nicholas II was the last tsar) manipulated the church elders. Mollie represents the self-centered bourgeoisie: she devotes herself to the most likely suppliers of luxuries and comfort.

The animals' original vision for their society stems from noble ideals. Orwell was a socialist himself and supported the creation of a government in which moral dignity and social equality would take precedence over selfish individual interests. The Russian revolutionaries began with such ideals as well; Marx certainly touted notions like these in his writings. On Animal Farm, however, as was the case in the Russian Revolution, power is quickly consolidated in the hands of those who devise, maintain, and participate in the running of society—the intelligentsia. This class of Russians and their allies quickly turned the Communist Party toward totalitarianism, an event mirrored in *Animal Farm* by the gradual assumption of power by the pigs. After Lenin's seizure of power, Communist Party leaders began jockeying for position and power, each hoping to seize control after Lenin's death. Snowball and Napoleon, whose power struggle develops fully in the next chapters, are based on two real Communist Party leaders: Snowball shares traits with the fiery, intelligent leader Leon Trotsky, while the lurking, subversive Napoleon has much in common with the later dictator Joseph Stalin.

Orwell's descriptions in this chapter of the pre-Rebellion misery of the farm animals serve his critique of social inequality and the mistreatment of workers. They also make a pointed statement about humans' abuse of animals. Indeed, the same impulse that led Orwell to sympathize with poor and oppressed human beings made him lament the cruelty that many human beings show toward other species. He got the idea for *Animal Farm* while watching a young boy whipping a cart-horse. His pity for the exploited horse reminded him of his sympathy for the exploited working class.

Orwell creates a particularly moving scene in portraying the animals' efforts to obliterate the painful reminders of their maltreatment: this episode stands out from much of the rest of the novella in its richness of detail. In the attention to "the bits, the nose-rings, the dog-chains, the cruel knives," and a whole host of other instruments of physical discipline, we see Orwell's profound empathy with the lowest of the low, as well as his intense hatred for physical suffering and its destruction of dignity.

CHAPTER III

"Four legs good, two legs bad."

(See QUOTATIONS, *p. 51*)

SUMMARY

The animals spend a laborious summer harvesting in the fields. The clever pigs think of ways for the animals to use the humans' tools, and every animal participates in the work, each according to his capacity. The resulting harvest exceeds any that the farm has ever known. Only Mollie and the cat shirk their duties. The powerful and hard-working Boxer does most of the heavy labor, adopting "I will work harder!" as a personal motto. The entire animal community reveres his dedication and strength. Of all of the animals, only Benjamin, the obstinate donkey, seems to recognize no change under the new leadership.

Every Sunday, the animals hold a flag-raising ceremony. The flag's green background represents the fields of England, and its white hoof and horn symbolize the animals. The morning rituals also include a democratic meeting, at which the animals debate and establish new policies for the collective good. At the meetings, Snowball and Napoleon always voice the loudest opinions, though their views always clash.

Snowball establishes a number of committees with various goals, such as cleaning the cows' tails and re-educating the rats and rabbits. Most of these committees fail to accomplish their aims, but the classes designed to teach all of the farm animals how to read and write meet with some success. By the end of the summer, all of the animals achieve some degree of literacy. The pigs become fluent in reading and writing, while some of the dogs are able to learn to read the Seven Commandments. Muriel the goat can read scraps of newspaper, while Clover knows the alphabet but cannot string the letters together. Poor Boxer never gets beyond the letter *D*. When it becomes apparent that many of the animals are unable to memorize the Seven Commandments, Snowball reduces the principles to one essential maxim, which he says contains the heart of Animalism: "Four legs good, two legs bad." The birds take offense until Snowball hastily explains that wings count as legs. The other animals accept the maxim without argument, and the sheep begin to chant it at random times, mindlessly, as if it were a song.

Napoleon takes no interest in Snowball's committees. When the dogs Jessie and Bluebell each give birth to puppies, he takes the puppies into his own care, saying that the training of the young should take priority over adult education. He raises the puppies in a loft above the harness room, out of sight of the rest of Animal Farm. Around this time, the animals discover, to their outrage, that the pigs have been taking all of the milk and apples for themselves. Squealer explains to them that pigs need milk and apples in order to think well, and since the pigs' work is brain work, it is in everyone's best interest for the pigs to eat the apples and drink the milk. Should the pigs' brains fail because of a lack of apples and milk, Squealer hints, Mr. Jones might come back to take over the farm. This prospect frightens the other animals, and they agree to forgo milk and apples in the interest of the collective good.

ANALYSIS

Boxer's motto, in response to the increased labors on Animal Farm, of "I will work harder" is an exact echo of the immigrant Jurgis Rudkus's motto, in response to financial problems, in Upton Sinclair's *The Jungle*. Whereas Boxer exerts himself for the common good, as his socialist society dictates he must, Jurgis exerts himself for his own good, as his capitalist society dictates he must. Both possess a blind faith that the key to happiness lies in conforming to the existing political-economic system. Committed to socialism, Orwell would almost certainly have read *The Jungle,* which, published in its entirety in 1906, was a searing indictment of capitalism and galvanized the American socialist movement. His appropriation of Jurgis's motto for Boxer implicitly links the oppression of capitalism with that of totalitarian communism, as, in each case, the state wholly ignores the suffering of those who strive to be virtuous and work within the system.

The varying degrees of literacy among the animals suggest the necessity of sharing information in order for freedom to be maintained. To the pigs' credit, they do try to teach the other animals the basics of reading and writing, but the other animals prove unable or unwilling. The result is a dangerous imbalance in knowledge, as the pigs become the sole guardians and interpreters of Animal Farm's guiding principles. The discrepancy among the animals' capacity for abstract thought leads the pigs to condense the Seven Commandments into one supreme slogan: "Four legs good, two legs bad." The birds' objection to the slogan points immediately to the phrase's excessive simplicity. Whereas the Seven Commandments that the pigs formulate are a detailed mix of antihuman directives ("No animal shall wear clothes"), moral value judgments ("No animal shall kill another animal"), and utopian ideals ("All animals are equal"), the new, reductive slogan contains none of these elements; it merely establishes a bold dichotomy that masks the pigs' treachery. The motto has undergone such generalization that it has become propaganda, a rallying cry that will keep the common animals focused on the pigs' rhetoric so that they will ignore their own unhappiness.

In its simplicity, this new, brief slogan is all too easy to understand and becomes ingrained in even the most dull-witted of minds, minds that cannot think critically about how the slogan, while seeming to galvanize the animals' crusade for freedom, actually enables the pigs to institute their own oppressive regime. The animals themselves may be partially responsible for this power imbalance: on the whole, they show little true initiative to learn—the dogs have no interest in reading anything but the Seven Commandments, and Benjamin decides not to put his ample reading skills to use. Though the birds don't understand Snowball's long-winded explanation of why wings count as legs, they accept it nonetheless, trusting in their leader. It would be unfair, however, to fault the common animals for their failure to realize that the pigs mean to oppress them. Their fervor in singing "Beasts of England" and willingness to follow the pigs' instructions demonstrate their virtuous desire to make life better for one another. The common animals cannot be blamed for their lesser intelligence. The pigs, however, mix their intelligence with ruthless guile and take advantage of the other animals' apathy. Their machinations are reprehensible.

Squealer figures crucially in the novel, as his proficiency in spreading lie-filled propaganda allows the pigs to conceal their acts of greed beneath a veneer of common good. His statements and behaviors exemplify the linguistic and psychological methods that the pigs use to control the other animals while convincing them that this strict regime is essential if the animals want to avoid becoming subject to human cruelty again. In the opinion of Orwell, the socialist goals of the Russian Revolution quickly became meaningless rhetorical tools used by the communists to control the people: the intelligentsia began to interpret the "good of the state" to mean the good of itself as a class, and anyone who opposed it was branded an "enemy of the people." On Animal Farm, Squealer makes himself useful to the other pigs by pretending to side with the oppressed animals and falsely aligning the common good with the good of the pigs.

CHAPTER IV

SUMMARY

By late summer, news of Animal Farm has spread across half the county. Mr. Jones lives ignominiously in Willingdon, drinking and complaining about his misfortune. Mr. Pilkington and Mr. Frederick, who own the adjoining farms, fear that disenchantment will spread among their own animals. Their rivalry with each other, however, prevents them from working together against Animal Farm. They merely spread rumors about the farm's inefficiency and moral reprehensibility. Meanwhile, animals everywhere begin singing "Beasts of England," which they have learned from flocks of pigeons sent by Snowball, and many begin to behave rebelliously.

At last, in early October, a flight of pigeons alerts Animal Farm that Mr. Jones has begun marching on the farm with some of Pilkington's and Frederick's men. Snowball, who has studied books about the battle campaigns of the renowned Roman general Julius Caesar, prepares a defense and leads the animals in an ambush on the men. Boxer fights courageously, as does Snowball, and the humans suffer a quick defeat. The animals' losses amount only to a single sheep, whom they give a hero's burial. Boxer, who believes that he has unintentionally killed a stable boy in the chaos, expresses his regret at taking a life, even though it is a human one. Snowball tells him not to feel guilty, asserting that "the only good human being is a dead one." Mollie, as is her custom, has avoided any risk to herself by hiding during the battle. Snowball and Boxer each receive medals with the inscription "Animal Hero, First Class." The animals discover Mr. Jones's gun where he dropped it in the mud. They place it at the base of the flagstaff, agreeing to fire it twice a year: on October 12th, the anniversary of the Battle of the Cowshed—as they have dubbed their victory—and on Midsummer's Day, the anniversary of the Rebellion.

ANALYSIS

This chapter extends the allegory of the Russian Revolution to Russia's interwar period. The spread of Animalism to surrounding farms evokes the attempts by Leon Trotsky to establish communism as an international movement. Trotsky believed, as did Karl Marx, that communism could only achieve its goals if implemented on a global scale, and he devoted much of his formidable intelligence and eloquence to setting off what Western leaders later called the "Domino Effect." The Domino Effect, or Domino Theory, posited that the conversion or "fall" of a noncommunist state to communism would precipitate the fall of other noncommunist governments in nearby states. Presidents Truman, Eisenhower, Kennedy, and Johnson used this theory to justify their military involvement in Greece, Turkey, and Vietnam—countries they hoped to "save" from the spread of communism. In *Animal Farm,* the proprietors of the neighboring farms fear a similar contagion, which we might term the "Snowball Effect." Just as the West tried to discredit Russian communism, so do Mr. Pilkington and Mr. Frederick spread disparaging rumors about Animal Farm. Just as diplomatic skirmishes between the West and Russia ended up bolstering Trotsky and his allies, the armed skirmish between humans and animals ends up strengthening the animals' hold on the farm.

In this chapter, Orwell makes masterful use of irony, an important component of satirical writing, to illustrate the gap between what the animals are fighting for and what they believe they are fighting for. All of the animals—except Mollie—fight their hardest in the Battle of the Cowshed, but as Chapter III demonstrates, they do not fully understand the ideals for which they fight, the principles that they defend. In putting all of their energies toward expelling the humans, the animals believe that they are protecting themselves from oppression. In reality, however, they are simply and unwittingly consolidating the pigs' power by muting the primary threat to the pigs' regime—the human menace. Moreover, though the animals are prepared to give their lives in defense of Animal Farm, they appear unprepared to deal with the consequences of their fight: Boxer is horrified when he thinks that he has killed the stable boy.

Snowball's emphatic declaration after the battle of the need for all animals "to be ready to die for Animal Farm" sets up Orwell's scrutiny of the motivations behind mass violence and manipulative leadership. Many readers have assumed that *Animal Farm,* in its critique of totalitarian communism, advocates the Western capitalist way of life as an alternative. Yet a closer reading suggests that Orwell may take a more complicated stance. For if the animals represent the Russian communists and the farmers represent noncommunist leaders, we see that Orwell denounces the communists, but also portrays the noncommunists in a very harsh light. Mr. Jones proves an irresponsible and neglectful farm owner, and neither Mr. Pilkington nor Mr. Frederick hesitates to quash violently any animal uprisings that threaten his own supremacy. There is nothing noble in the men's unprovoked attack on Animal Farm—they undertake this crusade merely out of self-interest.

Chapter V

> At this . . . nine enormous dogs wearing brass-studded collars came bounding into the barn. They dashed straight for Snowball. . . .
>
> *(See* QUOTATIONS, *p. 53)*

Summary

Mollie becomes an increasing burden on Animal Farm: she arrives late for work, accepts treats from men associated with nearby farms, and generally behaves contrary to the tenets of Animalism. Eventually she disappears, lured away by a fat, red-faced man who stroked her coat and fed her sugar; now she pulls his carriage. None of the other animals ever mentions her name again.

During the cold winter months, the animals hold their meetings in the big barn, and Snowball and Napoleon's constant disagreements continue to dominate the proceedings. Snowball proves a better speaker and debater, but Napoleon can better canvass for support in between meetings. Snowball brims with ideas for improving the farm: he studies Mr. Jones's books and eventually concocts a scheme to build a windmill, with which the animals could generate electricity and automate many farming tasks, bringing new comforts to the animals' lives. But building the windmill would entail much hard work and difficulty, and Napoleon contends that the animals should attend to their current needs rather than plan for a distant future. The question deeply divides the animals. Napoleon surveys Snowball's plans and expresses his contempt by urinating on them.

When Snowball has finally completed his plans, all assemble for a great meeting to decide whether to undertake the windmill project. Snowball gives a passionate speech, to which Napoleon responds with a pathetically unaffecting and brief retort. Snowball speaks further, inspiring the animals with his descriptions of the wonders of electricity. Just as the animals prepare to vote, however, Napoleon gives a strange whimper, and nine enormous dogs wearing brass-studded collars charge into the barn, attack Snowball, and chase him off the farm. They return to Napoleon's side, and, with the dogs growling menacingly, Napoleon announces that from now on meetings will be held only for ceremonial purposes. He states that all important decisions will fall to the pigs alone.

Afterward, many of the animals feel confused and disturbed. Squealer explains to them that Napoleon is making a great sacrifice in taking the leadership responsibilities upon himself and that, as the cleverest animal, he serves the best interest of all by making the decisions. These statements placate the animals, though they still question the expulsion of Snowball. Squealer explains that Snowball was a traitor and a criminal. Eventually, the animals come to accept this version of events, and Boxer adds greatly to Napoleon's prestige by adopting the maxims "I will work harder" and "Napoleon is always right." These two maxims soon reinforce each other when, three weeks after the banishment of Snowball, the animals learn that Napoleon supports the windmill project. Squealer explains that their leader never really opposed the proposal; he simply used his apparent opposition as a maneuver to oust the wicked Snowball. These tactics, he claims, served to advance the collective best interest. Squealer's words prove so appealing, and the growls of his three-dog entourage so threatening, that the animals accept his explanation without question.

ANALYSIS

This chapter illuminates Napoleon's corrupt and power-hungry motivations. He openly and unabashedly seizes power for himself, banishes Snowball with no justification, and shows a bald-faced willingness to rewrite history in order to further his own ends. Similarly, Stalin forced Trotsky from Russia and seized control of the country after Lenin's death. Orwell's experience in a persecuted Trotskyist political group in the late 1930s during the Spanish Civil War may have contributed to his comparatively positive portrayal of Snowball. Trotsky was eventually murdered in Mexico, but Stalin continued to evoke him as a phantom threat, the symbol of all enemy forces, when he began his bloody purges of the 1930s. These purges appear in allegorized form in the next chapters of *Animal Farm*.

Lenin once famously remarked that communism was merely socialism plus the electrification of the countryside, a comment that reveals the importance of technological modernization to leaders in the young Soviet Union. The centrality of the electrification projects in the Soviet Union inspired the inclusion of the windmill in *Animal Farm*. Communist leaders considered such programs absolutely essential for their new nation, citing their need to upgrade an infrastructure neglected by the tsars and keep up with the relatively advanced and increasingly hostile West. Russia devoted a great deal of brain- and manpower to putting these programs in place. As suggested by the plot of *Animal Farm*, Stalin initially balked at the idea of a national emphasis on modern technology, only to embrace such plans wholeheartedly once he had secured his position as dictator.

This chapter lies near the middle of Orwell's narrative and, in many ways, represents the climax of the tension that has been building from the beginning. Since the animals' initial victory over Mr. Jones, we have suspected the motives of the pig intelligentsia and Napoleon in particular: ever since the revelation in Chapter III that they have been stealing apples and milk for themselves, the pigs have appeared more interested in grabbing resources and power than in furthering the good of the farm. Now, when Napoleon sets his dogs on Snowball, he proves that his socialist rhetoric about the common good is quite empty. The specifics of Napoleon's takeover bespeak a long period of careful plotting: Napoleon has been deliberating his seizure of power ever since he first took control of the dogs' training, in Chapter III. Thus, the banishment of Snowball constitutes the culmination of long-held resentments and aspirations and climactically justifies our feelings of uneasiness about Napoleon.

In his use of the dogs, Napoleon has monopolized the farm's sources of defense and protection—the dogs could have guarded the farm and warded off predators—in order to create his own private secret police. The pigs claim a parallel monopoly on logic. Squealer linguistically transforms Napoleon's self-serving act of banishing Snowball into a supreme example of self-sacrifice and manages to convince the animals that no contradiction underlies the leader's abrupt about-face on the issue of the windmill. Each of Napoleon's acts of physical violence thus gains acceptance and legitimacy via a corresponding exercise of verbal violence. Political subversion depends on a subversion of logic and language. The connection between these two forms of violence and subversion remained a central concern for Orwell throughout his life, and he examines it both in later chapters of *Animal Farm* and in his last major novel, *1984*.

Chapter VI

Summary

For the rest of the year, the animals work at a backbreaking pace to farm enough food for themselves and to build the windmill. The leadership cuts the rations—Squealer explains that they have simply "readjusted" them—and the animals receive no food at all unless they work on Sunday afternoons. But because they believe what the leadership tells them—that they are working for their own good now, not for Mr. Jones's—they are eager to take on the extra labor. Boxer, in particular, commits himself to Animal Farm, doing the work of three horses but never complaining. Even though the farm possesses all of the necessary materials to build the windmill, the project presents a number of difficulties. The animals struggle over how to break the available stone into manageable sizes for building without picks and crowbars, which they are unable to use. They finally solve the problem by learning to raise and then drop big stones into the quarry, smashing them into usable chunks. By late summer, the animals have enough broken stone to begin construction.

Although their work is strenuous, the animals suffer no more than they had under Mr. Jones. They have enough to eat and can maintain the farm grounds easily now that humans no longer come to cart off and sell the fruits of their labor. But the farm still needs a number of items that it cannot produce on its own, such as iron, nails, and paraffin oil. As existing supplies of these items begin to run low, Napoleon announces that he has hired a human solicitor, Mr. Whymper, to assist him in conducting trade on behalf of Animal Farm. The other animals are taken aback by the idea of engaging in trade with humans, but Squealer explains that the founding principles of Animal Farm never included any prohibition against trade and the use of money. He adds that if the animals think that they recall any such law, they have simply fallen victim to lies fabricated by the traitor Snowball.

Mr. Whymper begins paying a visit to the farm every Monday, and Napoleon places orders with him for various supplies. The pigs begin living in the farmhouse, and rumor has it that they even sleep in beds, a violation of one of the Seven Commandments. But when Clover asks Muriel to read her the appropriate commandment, the two find that it now reads "No animal shall sleep in a bed with sheets." Squealer explains that Clover must have simply forgotten the last two words. All animals sleep in beds, he says—a pile of straw is a bed, after all. Sheets, however, as a human invention, constitute the true source of evil. He then shames the other animals into agreeing that the pigs need comfortable repose in order to think clearly and serve the greater good of the farm.

Around this time, a fearsome storm descends on Animal Farm, knocking down roof tiles, an elm tree, and even the flagstaff. When the animals go into the fields, they find, to their horror, that the windmill, on which they have worked so hard, has been toppled. Napoleon announces in appalled tones that the windmill has been sabotaged by Snowball, who, he says, will do anything to destroy Animal Farm. Napoleon passes a death sentence on Snowball, offering a bushel of apples to the traitor's killer. He then gives a passionate speech in which he convinces the animals that they must rebuild the windmill, despite the backbreaking toil involved. "Long live the windmill!" he cries. "Long live Animal Farm!"

ANALYSIS

Part of the greater importance of the novella owes to its treatment of Animal Farm not as an isolated entity but as part of a network of farms—an analogue to the international political arena. Orwell thus comments on Soviet Russia and the global circumstances in which it arose. But the tactics that we see the pigs utilizing here—the overworking of the laboring class, the justification of luxuries indulged in by the ruling class, the spreading of propaganda to cover up government failure or ineffectiveness—evoke strategies implemented not only by communist Russia but also by governments throughout the world needing to oppress their people in order to consolidate their power.

Napoleon makes the outrageous claim that Snowball was responsible for the windmill's destruction in order to shift the blame from his own shoulders. Governments throughout the world have long bolstered their standing among the populace by alluding to the horrors of an invisible, conspiratorial enemy, compared to which their own misdeeds or deficiencies seem acceptable. Stalin used this tactic in Russia by evoking a demonized notion of Trotsky, but the strategy has enjoyed popularity among many other administrations. Indeed, during much of the twentieth century, it was the communists who served as a convenient demon to governments in the West: both German and American governments used the threat of communism to excuse or cover up their own aggressive behaviors.

More broadly, the windmill represents the pigs' continued manipulation of the common animals. They not only force the animals to break their backs to construct the windmill by threatening to withhold food; they also use the windmill's collapse—the blame for which, though it is caused by a storm, rests with the pigs for not having the foresight to build thicker walls—to play on the animals' general fear of being re-enslaved. By deflecting the blame from themselves onto Snowball, they prevent the common animals from realizing how greatly the pigs are exploiting them and harness the animals' energy toward defeating this purported enemy.

In this chapter, Orwell also comments on the cyclical nature of tyranny. As the pigs gain power, they become increasingly corrupt. Soon they embody the very iniquity that Animal Farm was created to overturn. As many political observers have noted, Stalin and his officials quickly entered into the decadent lifestyles that had characterized the tsars. The communists themselves had pointed to these lifestyles in maligning the old administration. Orwell parodies this phenomenon by sketching his pigs increasingly along the lines of very grotesque human beings. Throughout the novel, the pigs increasingly resemble humans, eventually flouting altogether Old Major's strictures against adopting human characteristics. With the pigs' move into the farmhouse to sleep in the farmer's beds, Orwell remarks upon the way that supreme power corrupts all who possess it, transforming all dictators into ruthless, self-serving, and power-hungry entities that can subsist only by oppressing others.

CHAPTER VII

SUMMARY

In the bitter cold of winter, the animals struggle to rebuild the windmill. In January, they fall short of food, a fact that they work to conceal from the human farmers around them, lest Animal Farm be perceived to be failing. The humans refuse to believe that Snowball caused the destruction of the windmill, saying that the windmill's walls simply weren't thick enough. The animals deem this explanation false, but they nevertheless decide to build the walls twice as thick this time. Squealer gives ennobling speeches on the glory of sacrifice, but the other animals acquire their real inspiration from the example of Boxer, who works harder than ever. In order to feed the animals, Napoleon contracts to sell four hundred eggs a week. The other animals react with shock—one of Old Major's original complaints about humans focused on the cruelty of egg selling, or so they remember. The hens rebel, and Napoleon responds by cutting their rations entirely. Nine hens die before the others give in to Napoleon's demands.

Soon afterward, the animals hear, to their extreme dismay, that Snowball has been visiting the farm at night, in secret, and sabotaging the animals' efforts. Napoleon says that he can detect Snowball's presence everywhere, and whenever something appears to go wrong by chance, Snowball receives the blame. One day, Squealer announces that Snowball has sold himself to Mr. Frederick's farm, Pinchfield, and that the treacherous pig has been in league with Mr. Jones from the start. He recalls Snowball's attempts at the Battle of the Cowshed to have the animals defeated. The animals hear these words in stupefied astonishment. They remember Snowball's heroism and recall that he received a medal. Boxer, in particular, is completely baffled. But Napoleon and Squealer convince the others that Snowball's apparent bravery simply constituted part of his treacherous plot. They also work to convince the animals of Napoleon's superior bravery during that battle. So vividly does Squealer describe Napoleon's alleged heroic actions that the animals are almost able to remember them.

Four days later, Napoleon convenes all of the animals in the yard. With his nine huge dogs ringed about him and growling, he stages an inquisition and a purge: he forces certain animals to confess to their participation in a conspiracy with Snowball and then has the dogs tear out these supposed traitors' throats. The dogs, apparently without orders, even attack Boxer, who effortlessly knocks them away with his huge hooves. But four pigs and numerous other animals meet their deaths, including the hens who rebelled at the proposal to sell their eggs. The terrible bloodshed leaves the animals deeply shaken and confused. After Napoleon leaves, Boxer says that he would never have believed that such a thing could happen on Animal Farm. He adds that the tragedy must owe to some fault in the animals themselves; thus, he commits to working even harder. Clover looks out over the farm, wondering how such a glorious rebellion as theirs could have come to its current state. Some of the animals begin to sing "Beasts of England," but Squealer appears and explains that "Beasts of England" may no longer be sung. It applied only to the Rebellion, he says, and now there is no more need for rebellion. Squealer gives the animals a replacement song, written by Minimus, the poet pig. The new song expresses profound patriotism and glorifies Animal Farm, but it does not inspire the animals as "Beasts of England" once did.

ANALYSIS

The humans react with relief when the windmill topples because its failure seems to justify their contempt for the animals and their belief in their own superiority. Similarly, Soviet Russia struggled against a largely justified reputation for industrial incompetence, famine, and poor management. Stalin's vaunted Five-Year Plans for agriculture resulted in the starvation of millions of people, and industrial production lagged far behind the capitalist West. But the Soviets were determined to mask their problems and keep them from the eyes of the rest of the world. Correspondingly, the pigs of Animal Farm devise elaborate schemes to keep the human farmers from learning about their difficulties. The windmill becomes an important measure of the farm's competence, and its collapse deals a major blow to the pigs' prestige as equals in the community of farms—just as Soviet Russia's industrial setbacks threatened its position as an equal to the leading nations of the world and as a viable model of communist revolution.

Chapter VII joins Chapter VI in focusing primarily on the violent tactics employed by oppressive governments—again explored through the behavior of the pigs—to maintain the docility and obedience of the populace even as their economic and political systems falter and grow corrupt. In Soviet Russia, these tactics led to a massive class division in a supposedly egalitarian society. Orwell suggests that as long as a leadership claims a monopoly on logic, it will be able to justify its monopoly on resources, while the common people suffer and grow hungry. Similarly, as life on Animal Farm grows leaner and leaner for most of the animals, the pigs live in increasing luxury.

Napoleon's transformation of the exiled Snowball into a despicable enemy to all who care about the good of Animal Farm mirrors Stalin's abuse of the exiled Trotsky. Those animals who show even a glimmering of disapproval toward Napoleon, such as the hens who oppose the selling of their eggs, meet a swift death. Similarly, after forcing Trotsky's exile from Russia, Stalin continued to claim the existence of Trotskyist plots throughout Soviet society. During the 1930s, he staged a number of infamous "purges," show trials during which Stalin and his allies essentially forced government members and citizens to "confess" their complicity with Trotskyist or other anti-Stalinist conspiracies. In many cases, the purge victims would admit to activities in which they had never engaged, simply to put a stop to their torture. But after confessing, the alleged conspirators were executed as "enemies of the people." Stalin used his purges to eliminate any dissident elements in his government, provide his people with a common enemy to despise, and keep both the populace and his staff in a state of fear for their own safety, making them far less likely to disobey orders or challenge his rule in any way.

Just as the pigs rewrite history, they manipulate statistics in their favor, claiming that every important aspect of life on the farm has improved statistically since the Rebellion: animals live longer, eat more, have more offspring, work fewer hours, and so forth. In this way, the pigs produce a false vision of reality. Then, by ensuring that this reality is the only one to which the other animals have access and by establishing an effective death penalty for any animal who questions it, they render their dictatorship indestructible. Fear makes the animals inclined to believe the pigs' propaganda, and by allowing themselves to believe in the comforting lies, the animals find what may be their only safe haven from violence and terror.

Chapter VIII

Summary

A few days after the bloody executions, the animals discover that the commandment reading "No animal shall kill any other animal" now reads: "No animal shall kill any other animal without cause." As with the previous revisions of commandments, the animals blame the apparent change on their faulty memories—they must have forgotten the final two words. The animals work even harder throughout the year to rebuild the windmill. Though they often suffer from hunger and the cold, Squealer reads continuously from a list of statistics proving that conditions remain far superior to anything the animals knew under Mr. Jones and that they only continue to improve.

Napoleon has now taken the title of "Leader" and has dozens of other complimentary titles as well. Minimus has written a poem in praise of the Napoleon and inscribed it on the barn wall. A pile of timber lies unused on the farm, left over from the days of Mr. Jones, and Napoleon engages in complicated negotiations for the sale of it to either Mr. Frederick or Mr. Pilkington. When negotiations favor Mr. Frederick, the pigs teach the animals to hate Mr. Pilkington. When Mr. Pilkington then appears ready to buy the timber, the pigs teach the animals to hate Mr. Frederick with equal ferocity. Whichever farm is currently out of favor is said to be the hiding place of Snowball. Following a slew of propaganda against Mr. Frederick (during which Napoleon adopts the maxim "Death to Frederick!"), the animals are shocked to learn that Mr. Frederick eventually comes through as the buyer of the timber. The pigs talk endlessly about Napoleon's cleverness, for, rather than accept a check for the timber, he insists on receiving cash. The five-pound notes are now in his possession.

Soon the animals complete the construction of the windmill. But before they can put it to use, Napoleon discovers to his great outrage that the money Mr. Frederick gave him for the timber is simply a stack of forgeries. He warns the animals to prepare for the worst, and, indeed, Mr. Frederick soon attacks Animal Farm with a large group of armed men. The animals cower as Mr. Frederick's men plant dynamite at the base of the windmill and blow the whole structure up. Enraged, the animals attack the men, driving them away, but at a heavy cost: several of the animals are killed, and

Boxer sustains a serious injury. The animals are disheartened, but a patriotic flag-raising ceremony cheers them up and restores their faith somewhat.

Not long afterward, the pigs discover a crate of whisky in the farmhouse basement. That night, the animals hear singing and revelry from within, followed by the sound of a terrible quarrel. The next morning the pigs look bleary-eyed and sick, and the animals hear whisperings that Comrade Napoleon may be dying. By evening, however, he has recovered. The next night, some of the animals find Squealer near the barn, holding a paintbrush; he has fallen from a ladder leaned up against the spot where the Seven Commandments are painted on the barn. The animals fail to put two and two together, however, and when they discover that the commandment that they recall as stating "No animal shall drink alcohol" actually reads "No animal shall drink alcohol to excess," they once again blame their memories for being faulty.

ANALYSIS

By this point, Napoleon and Squealer have so systematically perverted the truth that the animals cannot recognize their leaders' duplicity even when they witness it directly. Karl Marx had theorized the need for a "dictatorship of the proletariat" during the early years of his prescribed revolution, under which democratic freedoms would take second place to stamping out resistance in the bourgeoisie. In Soviet Russia, Stalin and his colleagues used Marx's theories as a justification for their increasingly violent and tyrannical actions. Moreover, they used this one Marxist principle to justify their neglect of the other principles. The Stalinist government, for example, quickly altered the noble ideals of equal work and equal compensation in order to favor the politically and militarily powerful. Even when the machinations of the government became clear to everyone in Russia—in the novella we see such a moment when the animals catch Squealer literally rewriting the law on the side of the barn—no significant popular revolt among the working classes ever occurred. Similarly, the animals show no signs of rebellion.

Minimus's poem provides compelling evidence for the animals' largely uncritical attitude toward the regime that oppresses it. Though the poem is outrageously inflated and tastelessly sentimental, the animals don't question it; instead, they allow it to speak for them. With the poem, Orwell creates a passage of great irony and a wonderful satire of patriotic rhetoric. Much of the poem's humor arises from its combination of high and low language, exposing the ridiculousness of what it intends to celebrate. Thus, the poem praises Napoleon as "Fountain of happiness!" but also "Lord of the swill-bucket!" While it glorifies life under Napoleon, it emphasizes its simple triviality: "All that [his] creatures love" amounts to a "full belly" and "clean straw." This stylistic use of contrast helps render the poem's tone of utter devotion ("Oh how my soul is on / Fire") a mockery of itself. At the same time, of course, the poem parodies actual anthems and patriotic odes. Orwell aims to expose the inanity of such patriotic sentiment, and also its emptiness, if not its misdirection. He suggests that such rhetoric fails to examine the essence of that which it praises.

The description of Napoleon's dealings with his neighbors, Mr. Pilkington and Mr. Frederick, elaborately parodies Stalin's diplomatic tap dance with Germany and the Allies at the outset of World War II. Stalin, faced with an unpleasant choice between the capitalist Allies and the fascist Germans and reluctant to enter into another large war, stalled by alternately siding with one country and then the other, using propaganda to drag the populace along with his changing allegiances. At the last minute, and quite unexpectedly, he signed the Non-Aggression Pact (an agreement not to wage war on each other) with the German leader Adolf Hitler, much as Napoleon makes the surprise move of selling the timber to Mr. Frederick. Hitler almost immediately went back on his word—as is evoked by Mr. Frederick's forged banknotes—and invaded Russia's western frontier, eventually killing over twenty-five million Russians and demolishing much of the infrastructure that the Soviets had built since the Russian Revolution. In his depiction of the animals' response to Mr. Frederick's gratuitous destruction of the great windmill, Orwell aptly conveys the tremendous sense of betrayal and feelings of anger that Russians felt toward Germany during and after World War II.

The pigs, echoing another tactic of the victorious governments after World War II, use the heroism of individuals from the lower classes to reinforce the patriotism of the demoralized survivors. Orwell crafts particularly keen descriptions of the patriotic celebrations and rituals after the animals' war with Mr. Frederick's men. He subtly implies that while such ceremonies have the apparent function of bestowing the glory of the state upon the individual, they truly serve the opposite goal: to transfer the nobility of individual sacrifices onto the state.

There are several notable parallels between *Animal Farm* and Orwell's final novel, *1984*. One can argue that *Animal Farm* was even a sort of study for *1984*, which applies many of *Animal Farm*'s themes and ideas to human society, rendering the horror of totalitarian government all the more real. One of the principal ideas that each work addresses is the ability of those in power to control and alter both attitudes and history, especially by subverting language. Just as Squealer offers a host of statistics to show that Animal Farm is in better shape than ever, despite the fact that the animals are hungry and cold, so too does the Ministry of Plenty, in *1984*, crank out misleading reports about how greatly production has increased; indeed, the ministry reduces rations but convinces people that it is actually increasing them. Similarly, Animal Farm's ever-alternating alliance with Mr. Frederick and Mr. Pilkington and the leaders' claim that the farm has always remained committed to the same farmer reaches the apex of absurdity in *1984*. In the middle of a speech during Hate Week, the masses mindlessly accept the speaker's assertion that their country, Oceania, which has indeed been at war with Eurasia, is actually not at war and never has been at war with Eurasia. He says the country is and always has been at war with Eastasia. The masses, carrying explicit anti-Eurasia signs, become embarrassed about their apparent mistake.

CHAPTER IX

SUMMARY

Wearily and weakly, the animals set about rebuilding the windmill. Though Boxer remains seriously injured, he shows no sign of being in pain and refuses to leave his work for even a day. Clover makes him a poultice for his hoof, and he eventually does seem to improve, but his coat doesn't seem as shiny as before and his great strength seems slightly diminished. He says that his only goal is to see the windmill off to a good start before he retires. Though no animal has yet retired on Animal Farm, it had previously been agreed that all horses could do so at the age of twelve. Boxer now nears this age, and he looks forward to a comfortable life in the pasture as a reward for his immense labors.

Food grows ever more scarce, and all animals receive reduced rations, except for the pigs and the dogs. Squealer continues to produce statistics proving that, even with this "readjustment," the rations exceed those that they received under Mr. Jones. After all,

Squealer says, when the pigs and dogs receive good nourishment, the whole community stands to benefit. When four sows give birth to Napoleon's piglets, thirty-one in all, Napoleon commands that a schoolhouse be built for their education, despite the farm's dwindling funds. Napoleon begins ordering events called Spontaneous Demonstrations, at which the animals march around the farm, listen to speeches, and exult in the glory of Animal Farm. When other animals complain, the sheep, who love these Spontaneous Demonstrations, drown them out with chants of "Four legs good, two legs bad!"

In April, the government declares Animal Farm a republic, and Napoleon becomes president in a unanimous vote, having been the only candidate. The same day, the leadership reveals new discoveries about Snowball's complicity with Jones at the Battle of the Cowshed. It now appears that Snowball actually fought openly on Jones's side and cried "Long live Humanity!" at the outset of the fight. The battle took place so long ago, and seems so distant, that the animals placidly accept this new story. Around the same time, Moses the raven returns to the farm and once again begins spreading his stories about Sugarcandy Mountain. Though the pigs officially denounce these stories, as they did at the outset of their administration, they nonetheless allow Moses to live on the farm without requiring him to work.

One day, Boxer's strength fails; he collapses while pulling stone for the windmill. The other animals rush to tell Squealer, while Benjamin and Clover stay near their friend. The pigs announce that they will arrange to bring Boxer to a human hospital to recuperate, but when the cart arrives, Benjamin reads the writing on the cart's sideboards and announces that Boxer is being sent to a glue maker to be slaughtered. The animals panic and begin crying out to Boxer that he must escape. They hear him kicking feebly inside the cart, but he is unable to get out.

Soon Squealer announces that the doctors could not cure Boxer: he has died at the hospital. He claims to have been at the great horse's side as he died and calls it the most moving sight he has ever seen—he says that Boxer died praising the glories of Animal Farm. Squealer denounces the false rumors that Boxer was taken to a glue factory, saying that the hospital had simply bought the cart from a glue maker and had failed to paint over the lettering. The animals heave a sigh of relief at this news, and when Napoleon gives a great speech in praise of Boxer, they feel completely soothed.

Not long after the speech, the farmhouse receives a delivery from the grocer, and sounds of revelry erupt from within. The animals murmur among themselves that the pigs have found the money to buy another crate of whisky—though no one knows where they found the money.

ANALYSIS

As members of the revolutionary era in Russia began to expect to receive some compensation for all of the terrible sacrifices they had made in the revolution and in the war with Germany, they became painfully aware of the full extent of their betrayal at the hands of the Stalinist leadership. The quality of life for the average citizen continued to decline, even as the ruling class grew ever larger and consumed ever more luxuries. Orwell uses Boxer's death as a searing indictment of such totalitarian rule, and his death points sadly and bitterly to the downfall of Animal Farm. The great horse seems to have no bad qualities apart from his limited intellect, but, in the end, he falls victim to his own virtues—loyalty and the willingness to work. Thus, Boxer's great mistake lies in his conflation of the ideal of Animal Farm with the character of Napoleon: never thinking for himself about how the society should best realize its founding ideals, Boxer simply follows Napoleon's orders blindly, naïvely assuming that the pigs have the farm's best interest at heart. It is sadly ironic that the system that he so loyally serves ultimately betrays him: he works for the good of all but is sold for the good of the few.

The pig leadership's treachery and hypocrisy becomes even more apparent in the specific manner of Boxer's death: by selling Boxer for profit, the pigs reenact the very same cruelties against which the Rebellion first fights—the valuing of animals for their material worth rather than their dignity as living creatures. When a new crate of whisky arrives for the pigs, we can reasonably infer that the money for it has come from the sale of Boxer. Moreover, the intensely pathetic nature of Boxer's fate—death in a glue factory—contrasts greatly with his noble character, and the contrast contributes to the dramatic effect of Boxer's death, increasing the power of Orwell's critique. Boxer's life and death provide a microcosm for Orwell's conception of the ways in which the Russian communist power apparatus treated the working class that it purported to serve: Orwell suggests that the administration exhausted the resources of the workers for its own benefit and then mercilessly discarded them.

In order to defuse potential outrage at his blatant cruelty, Napoleon brings Moses back and allows him to tell his tales of Sugarcandy Mountain, much as Stalin made a place for the once-taboo Russian Orthodox Church after World War II. Moses's return signals the full return of oppression to the farm. While the pigs object early on to Moses's teachings because they undermine the animals' will to rebel, they now embrace the teachings for precisely the same reason. Napoleon further hopes to appease his populace by means of his Spontaneous Demonstrations, which force the animals to go through the motions of loyalty, despite what they may actually feel. The name of the new ritual bears particular irony: these gatherings are anything but spontaneous and demonstrate very little beyond a fearful conformity. The irony of the title indicates the overriding hollowness of the event.

Because the elite class controls the dissemination of information on Animal Farm, it is able to hide the terrible truth of its exploitation of the other animals. Fallible individual memories of Snowball's bravery and Napoleon's cowardice at the Battle of the Cowshed prove no match for the collective, officially sponsored memory that Squealer constructs, which paints a picture indicating completely the reverse. With no historical, political, or military resources at their command, the common animals have no choice but to go along with the charade.

CHAPTER X

> *All animals are equal, but some animals are more*
> *equal than others.*
>
> *(See* QUOTATIONS, *p. 54)*

SUMMARY

Years pass. Many animals age and die, and few recall the days before the Rebellion. The animals complete a new windmill, which is used not for generating electricity but for milling corn, a far more profitable endeavor. The farm seems to have grown richer, but only the many pigs and dogs live comfortable lives. Squealer explains that the pigs and dogs do very important work—filling out forms and such. The other animals largely accept this explanation, and their lives go on very much as before. They never lose their sense of pride in Animal Farm or their feeling that they have differentiated themselves from animals on other farms. The inhabitants of Animal Farm still fervently believe in the goals of the Rebellion—a world free from humans, with equality for all animals.

One day, Squealer takes the sheep off to a remote spot to teach them a new chant. Not long afterward, the animals have just finished their day's work when they hear the terrified neighing of a horse. It is Clover, and she summons the others hastily to the yard. There, the animals gaze in amazement at Squealer walking toward them on his hind legs. Napoleon soon appears as well, walking upright; worse, he carries a whip. Before the other animals have a chance to react to the change, the sheep begin to chant, as if on cue: "Four legs good, two legs better!" Clover, whose eyes are failing in her old age, asks Benjamin to read the writing on the barn wall where the Seven Commandments were originally inscribed. Only the last commandment remains: "all animals are equal." However, it now carries an addition: "but some animals are more equal than others." In the days that follow, Napoleon openly begins smoking a pipe, and the other pigs subscribe to human magazines, listen to the radio, and begin to install a telephone, also wearing human clothes that they have salvaged from Mr. Jones's wardrobe.

One day, the pigs invite neighboring human farmers over to inspect Animal Farm. The farmers praise the pigs and express, in diplomatic language, their regret for past "misunderstandings." The other animals, led by Clover, watch through a window as Mr. Pilkington and Napoleon toast each other, and Mr. Pilkington declares that the farmers share a problem with the pigs: "If you have your lower animals to contend with," he says, "we have our lower classes!" Mr. Pilkington notes with appreciation that the pigs have found ways to make Animal Farm's animals work harder and on less food than any other group of farm animals in the county. He adds that he looks forward to introducing these advances on his own farm. Napoleon replies by reassuring his human guests that the pigs never wanted anything other than to conduct business peacefully with their human neighbors and that they have taken steps to further that goal. Animals on Animal Farm will no longer address one another as "Comrade," he says, or pay homage to Old Major; nor will they salute a flag with a horn and hoof upon it. All of these customs have been changed recently by decree, he assures the men. Napoleon even announces that Animal Farm will now be known as the Manor Farm, which is, he believes, its "correct and original name."

The pigs and farmers return to their amiable card game, and the other animals creep away from the window. Soon the sounds of a quarrel draw them back to listen. Napoleon and Pilkington have played the ace of spades simultaneously, and each accuses the other of cheating. The animals, watching through the window, realize with a start that, as they look around the room of the farmhouse, they can no longer distinguish which of the cardplayers are pigs and which are human beings.

Analysis

> "If you have your lower animals to contend with," he said, "we have our lower classes!"
> *(See* QUOTATIONS, *p. 55)*

The last chapter of *Animal Farm* brings the novel to its logical, unavoidable, yet chilling conclusion. The pigs wholly consolidate their power and their totalitarian, communist dictatorship completely overwhelms the democratic-socialist ideal of Animal Farm. Napoleon and the other pigs have become identical to the human farmers, just as Stalin and the Russian communists eventually became indistinguishable from the aristocrats whom they had replaced and the Western capitalists whom they had denounced. The significance of Napoleon's name is now entirely clear: the historical Napoleon, who ruled France in the early nineteenth century and conquered much of Europe before being defeated at the Battle of Waterloo in 1814, originally appeared to be a great liberator, overthrowing Europe's kings and monarchs and bringing freedom to its people. But he eventually crowned himself emperor of France, shattering the dreams of European liberalism. Rather than destroying the aristocracy, Napoleon simply remade it around himself. Similarly, the pig Napoleon figures as the champion of Animalism early on. Now, however, he protests to the humans that he wants nothing more than to be one of them—that is, an oppressor.

Throughout the novella, Orwell has told his fable from the animals' point of view. In this chapter, we see clearly the dramatic power achieved by this narrative strategy. The animals remain naïvely hopeful up until the very end. Although they realize that the republic foretold by Old Major has yet to come to fruition, they stalwartly insist that it will come "[s]ome day." These assertions charge the final events of the story with an intense irony. For although Orwell has used foreshadowing and subtle hints to make us more suspicious than the animals of the pigs' motives, these statements of ingenuous faith in Animal Farm on the part of the common animals occur just before the final scene. This gap between the animals' optimism and the harsh reality of the pigs' totalitarian rule creates a sense of dramatic contrast. Although the descent into tyranny has been gradual, Orwell provides us with a restatement of the original ideals only moments before the full revelation of their betrayal.

Orwell uses emphatic one-line paragraphs to heighten the terror of this betrayal: the succinct conveyance of "It was a pig walking on his hind legs" and "He carried a whip in his trotter" drops this stunning information on us without warning, shocking us as much as it does the animals. Moreover, Orwell's decision to tell the story from the animals' point of view renders his final tableau all the more terrible. The picture of the pigs and farmers, indistinguishable from one another, playing cards together is disturbing enough by itself. Orwell, however, enables us to view this scene from the animals' perspective—from the outside looking in. By framing the scene in this way, Orwell points to the animals' total loss of power and entitlement: Animal Farm has not created a society of equals but has simply established a new class of oppressors to dominate the same class of oppressed—a division embodied, as at the opening of the novella, by the farmhouse wall.

The final distillation of the Seven Commandments that appears on the barn—"all animals are equal, but some are more equal than others"—stands as the last great example of how those in power manipulate language as an instrument of control. At the beginning of the novella, the idea of "more equal" would not only have seemed contrary to the egalitarian socialist spirit of Animal Farm, it would have seemed logically impossible. But after years of violence, hunger, dishonesty, and fear, the spirit of Animal Farm seems lost to a distant past. The concept of inherent equality has given way to notions of material entitlement: Animal Farm as an institution no longer values dignity and social justice; power alone renders a creature worthy of rights. By claiming to be "more equal"—an inherently nonsensical concept—than the other animals, the pigs have distorted the original ideals of the farm beyond recognition and have literally stepped into the shoes of their former tyrannical masters.

Important Quotations Explained

1. "Four legs good, two legs bad."

This phrase, which occurs in Chapter III, constitutes Snowball's condensation of the Seven Commandments of Animalism, which themselves serve as abridgments of Old Major's stirring speech on the need for animal unity in the face of human oppression. The phrase instances one of the novel's many moments of propagandizing, which Orwell portrays as one example of how the elite class abuses language to control the lower classes. Although the slogan seems to help the animals achieve their goal at first, enabling them to clarify in their minds the principles that they support, it soon becomes a meaningless sound bleated by the sheep ("two legs baa-d"), serving no purpose other than to drown out dissenting opinion. By the end of the novel, as the propagandistic needs of the leadership change, the pigs alter the chant to the similar-sounding but completely antithetical "Four legs good, two legs better."

2. Beasts of England, beasts of Ireland,
    Beasts of every land and clime,
    Hearken to my joyful tiding
    Of the golden future time.

These lines from Chapter I constitute the first verse of the song that
Old Major hears in his dream and which he teaches to the rest of the
animals during the fateful meeting in the barn. Like the communist
anthem "Internationale," on which it is based, "Beasts of England"
stirs the emotions of the animals and fires their revolutionary idealism. As it spreads rapidly across the region, the song gives the beasts
both courage and solace on many occasions. The lofty optimism of
the words "golden future time," which appear in the last verse as
well, serves to keep the animals focused on the Rebellion's goals so
that they will ignore the suffering along the way.

Later, however, once Napoleon has cemented his control over the
farm, the song's revolutionary nature becomes a liability. Squealer
chastises the animals for singing it, noting that the song was the
song of the Rebellion. Now that the Rebellion is over and a new
regime has gained power, Squealer fears the power of such idealistic,
future-directed lyrics. Wanting to discourage the animals' capacities
for hope and vision, he orders Minimus to write a replacement for
"Beasts of England" that praises Napoleon and emphasizes loyalty
to the state over the purity of Animalist ideology.

3. At this there was a terrible baying sound outside, and
    nine enormous dogs wearing brass-studded collars
    came bounding into the barn. They dashed straight for
    Snowball, who only sprang from his place just in time to
    escape their snapping jaws.

These words from Chapter V describe Napoleon's violent expulsion of Snowball from Animal Farm, which parallels the falling-out between Joseph Stalin and Leon Trotsky. Napoleon, who is clearly losing the contest for the hearts and minds of the lower animals to his rival Snowball, turns to his private police force of dogs to enforce his supremacy. As Stalin did, Napoleon prefers to work behind the scenes to build his power by secrecy and deception, while Snowball, as Trotsky did, devotes himself to winning popular support through his ideas and his eloquence. Napoleon's use of the attack dogs in this passage provides a blatant example of his differences with Snowball and points beyond the story to criticize real leaders for their use of such authoritarian tactics.

More generally, this episode is the first of many in which the political positioning of the Rebellion's early days gives way to overt violence, openly subverting the democratic principles of Animal Farm. It signals the deterioration of Animal Farm from a society based on equal rights to a society in which those who are powerful determine who gets what rights.

4.   All animals are equal, but some animals are more equal than others.

The ultimate example of the pigs' systematic abuse of logic and language to control their underlings, this final reduction of the Seven Commandments, which appears in Chapter X, clothes utterly senseless content in a seemingly plausible linguistic form. Although the first clause implies that all animals are equal to one another, it does not state this claim overtly. Thus, it is possible to misread the word "equal" as a relative term rather than an absolute one, meaning that there can be different degrees of "equal"-ness, just as there can be different degrees of colorfulness, for example (more colorful, less colorful). Once such a misreading has taken place, it becomes no more absurd to say "more equal" than to say "more colorful." By small, almost imperceptible steps like these, the core ideals of Animal Farm—and any human nation—gradually become corrupted.

The revision of the original phrase also points to the specific form of corruption on Animal Farm. The initial, unmodified phrase makes reference to all animals, its message extending to the entire world of animals without distinction. Similarly, Old Major expresses ideals that posit the dignity of all, the comradeship of all, the inclusion of all in voting and decision-making, so that no one group or individual will oppress another. The revised phrase, however, mentions an "all," but only in order to differentiate a "some" from that "all," to specify the uniqueness, the elite nature, and the chosen status of that "some." The pigs clearly envision themselves as this privileged "some"; under their totalitarian regime, the working animals exist only to serve the larger glory of the leadership, to provide the rulers with food and comfort, and to support their luxurious and exclusive lifestyle.

5.   "If you have your lower animals to contend with," he said,
      "we have our lower classes!"

This quip, delivered by Mr. Pilkington to Napoleon and his cabinet
during their well-catered retreat inside the farmhouse in Chapter X,
makes fully explicit the process of ideological corruption that has
been taking place throughout the novella. Old Major's notion of
the absolute division of interests between animals and humans here
gives way to a division between two classes, even cutting across species lines. Pigs and farmers share a need to keep down their laboring
classes. Mr. Pilkington's witticism lays bare the ugly but common
equation of laborers with animals.

   Moreover, the quote serves to emphasize directly the significance
of *Animal Farm* as a social commentary, cementing the conceptual
link between the downtrodden animals and the working classes of
the world. Orwell explodes his "fairy story," as he termed it, by
bringing it into the realm of human consequence, thereby making
its terrors all the more frightening to his readership.

KEY FACTS

FULL TITLE
Animal Farm: A Fairy Story

AUTHOR
George Orwell (pseudonym of Eric Arthur Blair)

TYPE OF WORK
Novella

GENRE
Dystopian animal fable; satire; allegory; political roman à clef (French for "novel with a key"—a thinly veiled exposé of factual persons or events)

LANGUAGE
English

TIME AND PLACE WRITTEN
1943–1944, in London

DATE OF FIRST PUBLICATION
1946

PUBLISHER
Harcourt Brace & Company

NARRATOR
Animal Farm is the only work by Orwell in which the author does not appear conspicuously as a narrator or major character; it is the least overtly personal of all of his writings. The anonymous narrator of the story is almost a nonentity, notable for no individual idiosyncrasies or biases.

POINT OF VIEW
The story is told from the point of view of the common animals of Animal Farm, though it refers to them in the third person plural as "they."

TONE
For the most part, the tone of the novel is objective, stating external facts and rarely digressing into philosophical meditations. The mixture of this tone with the outrageous

trajectory of the plot, however, steeps the story in an ever-mounting irony.

TENSE

Past

SETTING (TIME)

As is the case with most fables, *Animal Farm* is set in an unspecified time period and is largely free from historical references that would allow the reader to date the action precisely. It is fair to assume, however, that Orwell means the fable to be contemporaneous with the object of its satire, the Russian Revolution (1917–1945). It is important to remember that this period represented the recent past and present at the time of writing and that Orwell understands the significance of the story's action to be immediate and ongoing rather than historical.

SETTING (PLACE)

An imaginary farm in England

PROTAGONIST

There is no clear central character in the novel, but Napoleon, the dictatorial pig, is the figure who drives and ties together most of the action.

MAJOR CONFLICT

There are a number of conflicts in *Animal Farm*—the animals versus Mr. Jones, Snowball versus Napoleon, the common animals versus the pigs, Animal Farm versus the neighboring humans—but all of them are expressions of the underlying tension between the exploited and exploiting classes and between the lofty ideals and harsh realities of socialism.

RISING ACTION

The animals throw off their human oppressors and establish a socialist state called Animal Farm; the pigs, being the most intelligent animals in the group, take control of the planning and government of the farm; Snowball and Napoleon engage in ideological disputes and compete for power.

CLIMAX

In Chapter V, Napoleon runs Snowball off the farm with his trained pack of dogs and declares that the power to make decisions for the farm will be exercised solely by the pigs.

FALLING ACTION

Squealer emerges to justify Napoleon's actions with skillful but duplicitous reinterpretations of Animalist principles; Napoleon continues to consolidate his power, eliminating his enemies and reinforcing his status as supreme leader; the common animals continue to obey the pigs, hoping for a better future.

THEMES

The corruption of socialist ideals in the Soviet Union; the societal tendency toward class stratification; the danger of a naïve working class; the abuse of language as instrumental to the abuse of power

MOTIFS

Songs; state ritual

SYMBOLS

Animal Farm; the barn; the windmill

FORESHADOWING

The pigs' eventual abuse of power is foreshadowed at several points in the novel. At the end of Chapter II, immediately after the establishment of the supposedly egalitarian Animal Farm, the extra milk taken from the cows disappears, and the text implies that Napoleon has drunk it himself. Similarly, the dogs' attack on Boxer during Napoleon's purges, in Chapter VII, foreshadows the pigs' eventual betrayal of the loyal cart-horse.

KEY FACTS

STUDY QUESTIONS

1. *Compare and contrast Napoleon and Snowball. What*
    techniques do they use in their struggle for power?
    Does Snowball represent a morally legitimate political
    alternative to the corrupt leadership of Napoleon?

As Joseph Stalin did, Napoleon prefers to work behind the scenes
to build his power through manipulation and deal-making, while
Snowball devotes himself, as Leon Trotsky did, to winning popular support through his ideas, passionate speeches, and success in
debates with his opponent. Snowball seems to work within the political system, while Napoleon willingly circumvents it. Napoleon,
for instance, understands the role of force in political control, as is
made clear by his use of the attack dogs to expel Snowball from the
farm.

Despite Napoleon's clearly bullying tactics, Orwell's text doesn't
allow us to perceive Snowball as a preferable alternative. Snowball
does nothing to prevent the consolidation of power in the hands of
the pigs, nor does he stop the unequal distribution of goods in the
pigs' favor—he may even, in fact, be complicit in it early on. Furthermore, the ideals of Animal Farm—like Orwell's ideal version of
socialism—are rooted in democracy, with all of the animals decid-
ing how their collective action should be undertaken. For any one
animal to rise to greater power than any other would violate that
ideal and essentially render Animal Farm indistinguishable from a
human farm—an unavoidable eventuality by the end of the novella.
Though their motives for power may be quite different—Napoleon
seems to have a powerful, egocentric lust for control, while Snowball
seems to think himself a genius who should be the one to guide the
farm toward success—each represents a potential dictator. Neither
pig has the other animals' interests at heart, and thus neither represents the socialist ideals of Animal Farm.

2. *Why do you think Orwell chose to use a fable in his condemnation of Soviet communism and totalitarianism? Fiction would seem a rather indirect method of political commentary; if Orwell had written an academic essay, he could have named names, pointed to details, and proven his case more systematically. What different opportunities of expression does a fable offer its author?*

Historically, fables or parables have allowed writers to criticize individuals or institutions without endangering themselves: an author could always claim that he or she had aimed simply to write a fairy tale—a hypothetical, meaningless children's story. Even now, when many nations protect freedom of speech, fables still come across as less accusatory, less threatening. Orwell never condemns Stalin outright, a move that might have alienated certain readers, since Stalin proved an ally against Adolf Hitler's Nazi forces. Moreover, the language of a fable comes across as gentle, inviting, and unassuming: the reader feels drawn into the story and can follow the plot easily, rather than having to wade through a self-righteous polemic. In writing a fable, Orwell expands his potential audience and warms it to his argument before he even begins.

Because fables allow for the development of various characters, Orwell can use characterization to add an element of sympathy to his arguments. Especially by telling the story from the point of view of the animals, Orwell draws us in and allows us to identify with the working class that he portrays. Thus, a fable allows him to appeal more intensely to emotion than a political essay might enable him to do.

Additionally, in the case of *Animal Farm*, the lighthearted, pastoral, innocent atmosphere of the story stands in stark contrast to the dark, corrupt, malignant tendencies that it attempts to expose. This contrast adds to the story's force of irony: just as the idyllic setting and presentation of the story belies its wretched subject matter, so too do we see the utopian ideals of socialism give way to a totalitarian regime in which the lower classes suffer.

Finally, by writing in the form of a fable, Orwell universalizes his message. Although the specific animals and events that he portrays clearly evoke particular parallels in the real world, their status as symbols allows them to signify beyond specific times and places. Orwell himself encourages this breadth of interpretation: while the character of Napoleon, for example, refers most directly to Stalin in deed and circumstance, his name evokes his resemblance to the French general-turned-autocrat Napoleon.

3. *From whose perspective is* ANIMAL FARM *told? Why would Orwell have chosen such a perspective?*

Animal Farm is not told from any particular animal's perspective; properly speaking, it doesn't have a protagonist. Rather, it is told from the perspective of the common animals as a group: we read, for example, that "[t]he animals were stupefied. . . . It was some minutes before they could take it all in." This technique enables Orwell to paint a large portrait of the average people who suffer under communism. Through this choice of narrative perspective, he shows the loyalty, naïveté, gullibility, and work ethic of the whole class of common animals. In this way, he can effectively explore the question of why large numbers of people would continue to accept and support the Russian communist government, for example, even while it kept them hungry and afraid and even after its stated goals had clearly and decisively failed.

How to Write
Literary Analysis

The Literary Essay: A Step-by-Step Guide

When you read for pleasure, your only goal is enjoyment. You might find yourself reading to get caught up in an exciting story, to learn about an interesting time or place, or just to pass time. Maybe you're looking for inspiration, guidance, or a reflection of your own life. There are as many different, valid ways of reading a book as there are books in the world.

When you read a work of literature in an English class, however, you're being asked to read in a special way: you're being asked to perform *literary analysis*. To analyze something means to break it down into smaller parts and then examine how those parts work, both individually and together. Literary analysis involves examining all the parts of a novel, play, short story, or poem—elements such as character, setting, tone, and imagery—and thinking about how the author uses those elements to create certain effects.

A literary essay isn't a book review: you're not being asked whether or not you liked a book or whether you'd recommend it to another reader. A literary essay also isn't like the kind of book report you wrote when you were younger, where your teacher wanted you to summarize the book's action. A high school- or college-level literary essay asks, "How does this piece of literature actually work?" "How does it do what it does?" and, "Why might the author have made the choices he or she did?"

The Seven Steps
No one is born knowing how to analyze literature; it's a skill you learn and a process you can master. As you gain more practice with this kind of thinking and writing, you'll be able to craft a method that works best for you. But until then, here are seven basic steps to writing a well-constructed literary essay:

1. *Ask questions*
2. *Collect evidence*
3. *Construct a thesis*

65

4. Develop and organize arguments
5. Write the introduction
6. Write the body paragraphs
7. Write the conclusion

---

1. ASK QUESTIONS

When you're assigned a literary essay in class, your teacher will often provide you with a list of writing prompts. Lucky you! Now all you have to do is choose one. Do yourself a favor and pick a topic that interests you. You'll have a much better (not to mention easier) time if you start off with something you enjoy thinking about. If you are asked to come up with a topic by yourself, though, you might start to feel a little panicked. Maybe you have too many ideas—or none at all. Don't worry. Take a deep breath and start by asking yourself these questions:

- **What struck you?** Did a particular image, line, or scene linger in your mind for a long time? If it fascinated you, chances are you can draw on it to write a fascinating essay.

- **What confused you?** Maybe you were surprised to see a character act in a certain way, or maybe you didn't understand why the book ended the way it did. Confusing moments in a work of literature are like a loose thread in a sweater: if you pull on it, you can unravel the entire thing. Ask yourself why the author chose to write about that character or scene the way he or she did and you might tap into some important insights about the work as a whole.

- **Did you notice any patterns?** Is there a phrase that the main character uses constantly or an image that repeats throughout the book? If you can figure out how that pattern weaves through the work and what the significance of that pattern is, you've almost got your entire essay mapped out.

- **Did you notice any contradictions or ironies?** Great works of literature are complex; great literary essays recognize and explain those complexities. Maybe the title (*Happy Days*) totally disagrees with the book's subject matter (hungry orphans dying in the woods). Maybe the main character acts one way around his family and a completely different way around his friends and associates. If you can find a way to explain a work's contradictory elements, you've got the seeds of a great essay.

At this point, you don't need to know exactly what you're going to say about your topic; you just need a place to begin your exploration. You can help direct your reading and brainstorming by formulating your topic as a *question,* which you'll then try to answer in your essay. The best questions invite critical debates and discussions, not just a rehashing of the summary. Remember, you're looking for something you can *prove or argue* based on evidence you find in the text. Finally, remember to keep the scope of your question in mind: is this a topic you can adequately address within the word or page limit you've been given? Conversely, is this a topic big enough to fill the required length?

GOOD QUESTIONS

"Are Romeo and Juliet's parents responsible for the deaths of their children?"

"Why do pigs keep showing up in LORD OF THE FLIES*?"*

"Are Dr. Frankenstein and his monster alike? How?"

BAD QUESTIONS

"What happens to Scout in TO KILL A MOCKINGBIRD*?"*

"What do the other characters in JULIUS CAESAR *think about Caesar?"*

"How does Hester Prynne in THE SCARLET LETTER *remind me of my sister?"*

---

2. COLLECT EVIDENCE

Once you know what question you want to answer, it's time to scour the book for things that will help you answer the question. Don't worry if you don't know what you want to say yet—right now you're just collecting ideas and material and letting it all percolate. Keep track of passages, symbols, images, or scenes that deal with your topic. Eventually, you'll start making connections between these examples and your thesis will emerge.

Here's a brief summary of the various parts that compose each and every work of literature. These are the elements that you will analyze in your essay, and which you will offer as evidence to support your arguments. For more on the parts of literary works, see the Glossary of Literary Terms at the end of this section.

LITERARY ANALYSIS

ELEMENTS OF STORY   These are the *what*s of the work—what happens, where it happens, and to whom it happens.

- **Plot:** All of the events and actions of the work.

- **Character:** The people who act and are acted upon in a literary work. The main character of a work is known as the *protagonist*.

- **Conflict:** The central tension in the work. In most cases, the protagonist wants something, while opposing forces (antagonists) hinder the protagonist's progress.

- **Setting:** When and where the work takes place. Elements of setting include location, time period, time of day, weather, social atmosphere, and economic conditions.

- **Narrator:** The person telling the story. The narrator may straightforwardly report what happens, convey the subjective opinions and perceptions of one or more characters, or provide commentary and opinion in his or her own voice.

- **Themes:** The main idea or message of the work—usually an abstract idea about people, society, or life in general. A work may have many themes, which may be in tension with one another.

ELEMENTS OF STYLE   These are the *how*s—how the characters speak, how the story is constructed, and how language is used throughout the work.

- **Structure and organization:** How the parts of the work are assembled. Some novels are narrated in a linear, chronological fashion, while others skip around in time. Some plays follow a traditional three- or five-act structure, while others are a series of loosely connected scenes. Some authors deliberately leave gaps in their works, leaving readers to puzzle out the missing information. A work's structure and organization can tell you a lot about the kind of message it wants to convey.

- **Point of view:** The perspective from which a story is told. In *first-person point of view*, the narrator involves him or herself in the story. ("I went to the store"; "We watched in horror as the bird slammed into the window.") A first-person narrator is usually the protagonist of the work, but not always. In *third-person point of view*, the narrator does not participate in the story. A third-person narrator may closely follow a specific character, recounting that individual character's thoughts or experiences, or it may be what we call an *omniscient* narrator. Omniscient narrators see and know all: they can witness any event in any time or place and are privy to the inner thoughts and feelings of all characters. Remember that the narrator and the author are not the same thing!

- **Diction:** Word choice. Whether a character uses dry, clinical language or flowery prose with lots of exclamation points can tell you a lot about his or her attitude and personality.

- **Syntax:** Word order and sentence construction. Syntax is a crucial part of establishing an author's narrative voice. Ernest Hemingway, for example, is known for writing in very short, straightforward sentences, while James Joyce characteristically wrote in long, incredibly complicated lines.

- **Tone:** The mood or feeling of the text. Diction and syntax often contribute to the tone of a work. A novel written in short, clipped sentences that use small, simple words might feel brusque, cold, or matter-of-fact.

- **Imagery:** Language that appeals to the senses, representing things that can be seen, smelled, heard, tasted, or touched.

- **Figurative language:** Language that is not meant to be interpreted literally. The most common types of figurative language are *metaphors* and *similes,* which compare two unlike things in order to suggest a similarity between them— for example, "All the world's a stage," or "The moon is like a ball of green cheese." (Metaphors say one thing *is* another thing; similes claim that one thing is *like* another thing.)

---

3. CONSTRUCT A THESIS
When you've examined all the evidence you've collected and know how you want to answer the question, it's time to write your thesis statement. A *thesis* is a claim about a work of literature that needs to be supported by evidence and arguments. The thesis statement is the heart of the literary essay, and the bulk of your paper will be spent trying to prove this claim. A good thesis will be:

- **Arguable.** "*The Great Gatsby* describes New York society in the 1920s" isn't a thesis—it's a fact.

- **Provable through textual evidence**. "*Hamlet* is a confusing but ultimately very well-written play" is a weak thesis because it offers the writer's personal opinion about the book. Yes, it's arguable, but it's not a claim that can be proved or supported with examples taken from the play itself.
- **Surprising**. "Both George and Lenny change a great deal in *Of Mice and Men*" is a weak thesis because it's obvious. A really strong thesis will argue for a reading of the text that is not immediately apparent.
- **Specific**. "Dr. Frankenstein's monster tells us a lot about the human condition" is *almost* a really great thesis statement, but it's still too vague. What does the writer mean by "a lot"? *How* does the monster tell us so much about the human condition?

GOOD THESIS STATEMENTS

Question: In *Romeo and Juliet*, which is more powerful in shaping the lovers' story: fate or foolishness?

Thesis: "Though Shakespeare defines Romeo and Juliet as 'star-crossed lovers' and images of stars and planets appear throughout the play, a closer examination of that celestial imagery reveals that the stars are merely witnesses to the characters' foolish activities and not the causes themselves."

Question: How does the bell jar function as a symbol in Sylvia Plath's *The Bell Jar*?

Thesis: "A bell jar is a bell-shaped glass that has three basic uses: to hold a specimen for observation, to contain gases, and to maintain a vacuum. The bell jar appears in each of these capacities in *The Bell Jar*, Plath's semi-autobiographical novel, and each appearances marks a different stage in Esther's mental breakdown."

Question: Would Piggy in *The Lord of the Flies* make a good island leader if he were given the chance?

Thesis: "Though the intelligent, rational, and innovative Piggy has the mental characteristics of a good leader, he ultimately lacks the social skills necessary to be an effective one. Golding emphasizes this point by giving Piggy a foil in the charismatic Jack, whose magnetic personality allows him to capture and wield power effectively, if not always wisely."

4. DEVELOP AND ORGANIZE ARGUMENTS

The reasons and examples that support your thesis will form the middle paragraphs of your essay. Since you can't really write your thesis statement until you know how you'll structure your argument, you'll probably end up working on steps 3 and 4 at the same time.

There's no single method of argumentation that will work in every context. One essay prompt might ask you to compare and contrast two characters, while another asks you to trace an image through a given work of literature. These questions require different kinds of answers and therefore different kinds of arguments. Below, we'll discuss three common kinds of essay prompts and some strategies for constructing a solid, well-argued case.

TYPES OF LITERARY ESSAYS

- **Compare and contrast**

  Compare and contrast the characters of Huck and Jim in THE ADVENTURES OF HUCKLEBERRY FINN.

  Chances are you've written this kind of essay before. In an academic literary context, you'll organize your arguments the same way you would in any other class. You can either go *subject by subject* or *point by point*. In the former, you'll discuss one character first and then the second. In the latter, you'll choose several traits (attitude toward life, social status, images and metaphors associated with the character) and devote a paragraph to each. You may want to use a mix of these two approaches—for example, you may want to spend a paragraph a piece broadly sketching Huck's and Jim's personalities before transitioning into a paragraph or two that describes a few key points of comparison. This can be a highly effective strategy if you want to make a counterintuitive argument—that, despite seeming to be totally different, the two objects being compared are actually similar in a very important way (or vice versa). Remember that your essay should reveal something fresh or unexpected about the text, so think beyond the obvious parallels and differences.

- **Trace**

  Choose an image—for example, birds, knives, or eyes—and trace that image throughout MACBETH.

  Sounds pretty easy, right? All you need to do is read the play, underline every appearance of a knife in *Macbeth*, and then list them in your essay in the order they appear, right? Well, not exactly. Your teacher doesn't want a simple catalog of examples. He or she wants to see you make *connections* between those examples—that's the difference between summarizing and analyzing. In the *Macbeth* example above, think about the different contexts in which knives appear in the play and to what effect. In *Macbeth,* there are real knives and imagined knives; knives that kill and knives that simply threaten. Categorize and classify your examples to give them some order. Finally, always keep the overall effect in mind. After you choose and analyze your examples, you should come to some greater understanding about the work, as well as your chosen image, symbol, or phrase's role in developing the major themes and stylistic strategies of that work.

- **Debate**

  Is the society depicted in 1984 good for its citizens?

  In this kind of essay, you're being asked to debate a moral, ethical, or aesthetic issue regarding the work. You might be asked to judge a character or group of characters (*Is Caesar responsible for his own demise?*) or the work itself (*Is JANE EYRE a feminist novel?*). For this kind of essay, there are two important points to keep in mind. First, don't simply base your arguments on your personal feelings and reactions. Every literary essay expects you to read and analyze the work, so search for evidence in the text. What do characters in *1984* have to say about the government of Oceania? What images does Orwell use that might give you a hint about his attitude toward the government? As in any debate, you also need to make sure that you define all the necessary terms before you begin to argue your case. What does it mean to be a "good" society? What makes a novel "feminist"? You should define your terms right up front, in the first paragraph after your introduction.

  Second, remember that strong literary essays make contrary and surprising arguments. Try to think outside the box. In the *1984* example above, it seems like the obvious answer would be no, the totalitarian society depicted in Orwell's novel is *not* good for its citizens. But can you think of any arguments for the opposite side? Even if your final assertion is that the novel depicts a cruel, repressive, and therefore harmful society, acknowledging and responding to the counterargument will strengthen your overall case.

5. WRITE THE INTRODUCTION

Your introduction sets up the entire essay. It's where you present your topic and articulate the particular issues and questions you'll be addressing. It's also where you, as the writer, introduce yourself to your readers. A persuasive literary essay immediately establishes its writer as a knowledgeable, authoritative figure.

An introduction can vary in length depending on the overall length of the essay, but in a traditional five-paragraph essay it should be no longer than one paragraph. However long it is, your introduction needs to:

- **Provide any necessary context.** Your introduction should situate the reader and let him or her know what to expect. What book are you discussing? Which characters? What topic will you be addressing?

- **Answer the "So what?" question.** Why is this topic important, and why is your particular position on the topic noteworthy? Ideally, your introduction should pique the reader's interest by suggesting how your argument is surprising or otherwise counterintuitive. Literary essays make unexpected connections and reveal less-than-obvious truths.

- **Present your thesis.** This usually happens at or very near the end of your introduction.

- **Indicate the shape of the essay to come.** Your reader should finish reading your introduction with a good sense of the scope of your essay as well as the path you'll take toward proving your thesis. You don't need to spell out every step, but you do need to suggest the organizational pattern you'll be using.

Your introduction should not:

- **Be vague.** Beware of the two killer words in literary analysis: *interesting* and *important*. Of course the work, question, or example is interesting and important—that's why you're writing about it!

- **Open with any grandiose assertions.** Many student readers think that beginning their essays with a flamboyant statement such as, "Since the dawn of time, writers have been fascinated with the topic of free will," makes them sound important and commanding. You know what? It actually sounds pretty amateurish.

- **Wildly praise the work.** Another typical mistake student writers make is extolling the work or author. Your teacher doesn't need to be told that "Shakespeare is perhaps the greatest writer in the English language." You can mention a work's reputation in passing—by referring to *The Adventures of Huckleberry Finn* as "Mark Twain's enduring classic," for example—but don't make a point of bringing it up unless that reputation is key to your argument.

- **Go off-topic.** Keep your introduction streamlined and to the point. Don't feel the need to throw in all kinds of bells and whistles in order to impress your reader—just get to the point as quickly as you can, without skimping on any of the required steps.

---

6. WRITE THE BODY PARAGRAPHS

Once you've written your introduction, you'll take the arguments you developed in step 4 and turn them into your body paragraphs. The organization of this middle section of your essay will largely be determined by the argumentative strategy you use, but no matter how you arrange your thoughts, your body paragraphs need to do the following:

- **Begin with a strong topic sentence.** Topic sentences are like signs on a highway: they tell the reader where they are and where they're going. A good topic sentence not only alerts readers to what issue will be discussed in the following paragraph but also gives them a sense of what argument will be made *about* that issue. "Rumor and gossip play an important role in *The Crucible*" isn't a strong topic sentence because it doesn't tell us very much. "The community's constant gossiping creates an environment that allows false accusations to flourish" is a much stronger topic sentence— it not only tells us *what* the paragraph will discuss (gossip) but *how* the paragraph will discuss the topic (by showing how gossip creates a set of conditions that leads to the play's climactic action).

- **Fully and completely develop a single thought.** Don't skip around in your paragraph or try to stuff in too much material. Body paragraphs are like bricks: each individual

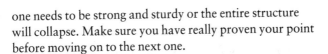

one needs to be strong and sturdy or the entire structure will collapse. Make sure you have really proven your point before moving on to the next one.

- **Use transitions effectively.** Good literary essay writers know that each paragraph must be clearly and strongly linked to the material around it. Think of each paragraph as a response to the one that precedes it. Use transition words and phrases such as *however, similarly, on the contrary, therefore,* and *furthermore* to indicate what kind of response you're making.

---

7. Write the Conclusion

Just as you used the introduction to ground your readers in the topic before providing your thesis, you'll use the conclusion to quickly summarize the specifics learned thus far and then hint at the broader implications of your topic. A good conclusion will:

- **Do more than simply restate the thesis.** If your thesis argued that *The Catcher in the Rye* can be read as a Christian allegory, don't simply end your essay by saying, "And that is why *The Catcher in the Rye* can be read as a Christian allegory." If you've constructed your arguments well, this kind of statement will just be redundant.

- **Synthesize the arguments, not summarize them.** Similarly, don't repeat the details of your body paragraphs in your conclusion. The reader has already read your essay, and chances are it's not so long that they've forgotten all your points by now.

- **Revisit the "So what?" question.** In your introduction, you made a case for why your topic and position are important. You should close your essay with the same sort of gesture. What do your readers know now that they didn't know before? How will that knowledge help them better appreciate or understand the work overall?

- **Move from the specific to the general.** Your essay has most likely treated a very specific element of the work—a single character, a small set of images, or a particular passage. In your conclusion, try to show how this narrow discussion has wider implications for the work overall. If your essay on *To Kill a Mockingbird* focused on the character of Boo Radley, for example, you might want to include a bit in your conclusion about how he fits into the novel's larger message about childhood, innocence, or family life.

- **Stay relevant.** Your conclusion should suggest new directions of thought, but it shouldn't be treated as an opportunity to pad your essay with all the extra, interesting ideas you came up with during your brainstorming sessions but couldn't fit into the essay proper. Don't attempt to stuff in unrelated queries or too many abstract thoughts.

- **Avoid making overblown closing statements.** A conclusion should open up your highly specific, focused discussion, but it should do so without drawing a sweeping lesson about life or human nature. Making such observations may be part of the point of reading, but it's almost always a mistake in essays, where these observations tend to sound overly dramatic or simply silly.

A+ Essay Checklist

Congratulations! If you've followed all the steps we've outlined above, you should have a solid literary essay to show for all your efforts. What if you've got your sights set on an A+? To write the kind of superlative essay that will be rewarded with a perfect grade, keep the following rubric in mind. These are the qualities that teachers expect to see in a truly A+ essay. How does yours stack up?

- ✓ Demonstrates a thorough understanding of the book
- ✓ Presents an original, compelling argument
- ✓ Thoughtfully analyzes the text's formal elements
- ✓ Uses appropriate and insightful examples
- ✓ Structures ideas in a logical and progressive order
- ✓ Demonstrates a mastery of sentence construction, transitions, grammar, spelling, and word choice

Suggested Essay Topics

1. *Discuss Boxer. What role does he play on the farm? Why does Napoleon seem to feel threatened by him? In what ways might one view the betrayal of Boxer as an alternative climax of the novel (if we consider Napoleon's banishment of Snowball and the pigs' initial consolidation of power as the true climax)?*

2. *Do you think ANIMAL FARM's message would come across effectively to someone who knows nothing about Soviet history or the conflict between Stalin and Trotsky? What might such a reader make of the story?*

3. *Of all of the characters in ANIMAL FARM, are there any who seem to represent the point of view of the author? Which of the animals or people do you think come(s) closest to achieving Orwell's perspective on ANIMAL FARM?*

A+ Student Essay

How do the pigs maintain their authority on Animal Farm?

George Orwell's *Animal Farm* examines the insidious ways in which public officials can abuse their power, as it depicts a society in which democracy dissolves into autocracy and finally into totalitarianism. From the Rebellion onward, the pigs of Animal Farm use violence and the threat of violence to control the other animals. However, while the attack dogs keep the other animals in line, physical intimidation doesn't prevent some of them from quietly questioning Napoleon's decisions. To check this threat to the pigs' power, Napoleon relies on rousing slogans, songs, and phrases to instill patriotism and conformity among the animals. On Animal Farm, it quickly becomes clear that language and rhetoric can be much more effective tools of social control than violence.

The pigs rely on slogans, poems, and commandments to both inspire the animals and keep them subservient. Crucially, the pigs understand that their songs and sayings must be easy to memorize and repeat if the other animals are to internalize their precepts. When written commandments prove too difficult for many of the animals, the pigs synthesize them into a single, brief catchphrase: "Four legs good, two legs bad." The slogan inspires the animals to adore their leaders rather than fear them, and by repeating it they deepen their commitment to the pigs. Boxer, the loyal cart-horse, continuously reaffirms his faith in the pigs' judgment by repeating the slogan "Napoleon is always right" in addition to his usual mantra, "I will work harder." The animals eventually use the pigs' slogans to police themselves, such as when several animals protest Napoleon's decision to begin trading farm products to humans. Though they are initially silenced by "a tremendous growling from the dogs," the tension isn't dissolved until the sheep break into a collective recital of "'Four legs good, two legs bad!'" In this key scene, Orwell explicitly contrasts brute force and the power of language, demonstrating that while the former may be effective in the short term, the latter has deeper, more lasting effects. The central role of rhetoric in the pigs' administration is illustrated by the power afforded Squealer, the aptly-named spokespig, as well as the presence of a government poet pig, Minimus.

In addition to the songs, slogans, poems, and commandments, Napoleon and the pigs also rewrite the oral and written histories of the farm in order to serve their needs and maintain their authority. When Napoleon violently seizes power, he quickly justifies his take-over by falsely denouncing his former ally and fellow revolution-ary, Snowball, as a human-sympathizer and enemy of Animalism. In fact, he continuously retells the story of Snowball's "treachery" until Snowball's role in the Rebellion and subsequent founding of Animal Farm has been completely effaced. Despite the fact that many of the animals remember Snowball receiving a medal for his bravery in the Battle of the Cowshed, Squealer convinces them that Snowball had actually fought alongside Mr. Jones against the animals. Loyal Boxer, who has trouble believing the official tale, is convinced otherwise when Squealer tells him that Napoleon knows it to be true. "Ah, that is different," exclaims Boxer. "If Comrade Napoleon says it, it must be right." Later, as the pigs move into the farmhouse, Squealer makes more revisions to the official doc-trine when he secretly amends the commandment "No animal shall sleep in a bed" to "No animal shall sleep in a bed *with sheets*" and revises the rule about drinking to "No animal shall drink alco-hol *to excess*." The pigs even replace the old mantras with "Four legs good, two legs *better*," and ultimately, "All animals are equal, except some are more equal than others." When the animals actu-ally catch Squealer in the act of rewriting the commandments, they don't seriously suspect anything, a testament to the power the pigs' rhetoric and language has over them.

The pigs' slogans and catchphrases have brainwashed the other animals to such an extent that even when the dogs slaughter doz-ens of animals for supposedly having colluded with Snowball, they don't question Napoleon's leadership. Although unsettled, their misgivings melt away as soon as the sheep chime in with "their usual bleating" of Animal Farm's primary maxim, "'Four legs good, two legs bad,'" which they chant for "several minutes" until the possi-bility of discussion has passed. Of course, not all political rhetoric is categorically bad—we see the rousing affect Old Major's song "The Beasts of England" has on the animals and how it prompts them to overthrow the tyrant Farmer Jones and create their own govern-ment. Orwell argues, however, that language can be used just as effectively for more sinister purposes, as a device of social manipu-lation and control, and that such rhetoric is often far more powerful than state-sanctioned violence or the threat of physical force.

GLOSSARY OF LITERARY TERMS

ANTAGONIST

The entity that acts to frustrate the goals of the *protagonist*. The antagonist is usually another *character* but may also be a non-human force.

ANTIHERO / ANTIHEROINE

A *protagonist* who is not admirable or who challenges notions of what should be considered admirable.

CHARACTER

A person, animal, or any other thing with a personality that appears in a *narrative*.

CLIMAX

The moment of greatest intensity in a text or the major turning point in the *plot*.

CONFLICT

The central struggle that moves the *plot* forward. The conflict can be the *protagonist*'s struggle against fate, nature, society, or another person.

FIRST-PERSON POINT OF VIEW

A literary style in which the *narrator* tells the story from his or her own *point of view* and refers to himself or herself as "I." The narrator may be an active participant in the story or just an observer.

HERO / HEROINE

The principal *character* in a literary work or *narrative*.

IMAGERY

Language that brings to mind sense-impressions, representing things that can be seen, smelled, heard, tasted, or touched.

MOTIF

A recurring idea, structure, contrast, or device that develops or informs the major *themes* of a work of literature.

NARRATIVE

A story.

NARRATOR
The person (sometimes a *character*) who tells a story; the *voice* assumed by the writer. The narrator and the author of the work of literature are not the same person.

PLOT
The arrangement of the events in a story, including the sequence in which they are told, the relative emphasis they are given, and the causal connections between events.

POINT OF VIEW
The *perspective* that a *narrative* takes toward the events it describes.

PROTAGONIST
The main *character* around whom the story revolves.

SETTING
The location of a *narrative* in time and space. Setting creates mood or atmosphere.

SUBPLOT
A secondary *plot* that is of less importance to the overall story but may serve as a point of contrast or comparison to the main plot.

SYMBOL
An object, *character,* figure, or color that is used to represent an abstract idea or concept. Unlike an *emblem,* a symbol may have different meanings in different contexts.

SYNTAX
The way the words in a piece of writing are put together to form lines, phrases, or clauses; the basic structure of a piece of writing.

THEME
A fundamental and universal idea explored in a literary work.

TONE
The author's attitude toward the subject or *characters* of a story or poem or toward the reader.

VOICE
An author's individual way of using language to reflect his or her own personality and attitudes. An author communicates voice through *tone, diction,* and *syntax.*

A Note on Plagiarism

Plagiarism—presenting someone else's work as your own—rears its ugly head in many forms. Many students know that copying text without citing it is unacceptable. But some don't realize that even if you're not quoting directly, but instead are paraphrasing or summarizing, *it is plagiarism* unless you cite the source.

Here are the most common forms of plagiarism:

- Using an author's phrases, sentences, or paragraphs without citing the source
- Paraphrasing an author's ideas without citing the source
- Passing off another student's work as your own

How do you steer clear of plagiarism? You should *always* acknowledge all words and ideas that aren't your own by using quotation marks around verbatim text or citations like footnotes and endnotes to note another writer's ideas. For more information on how to give credit when credit is due, ask your teacher for guidance or visit www.sparknotes.com.

Review & Resources

Quiz

1. Which animal hides during the Battle of the Cowshed?

   A. Boxer
   B. Clover
   C. Jessie
   D. Mollie

2. To whom does Napoleon sell the farm's pile of timber?

   A. Mr. Pilkington
   B. Mr. Frederick
   C. Mr. Jones
   D. Snowball

3. How does Napoleon express his contempt for Snowball's windmill plans?

   A. By spitting on them
   B. By giving a scathing speech
   C. By urinating on them
   D. By writing Snowball a letter

4. Who reduces the ideals of Animalism to the phrase "Four legs good, two legs bad"?

   A. Snowball
   B. Napoleon
   C. Squealer
   D. Boxer

5. Who teaches the sheep to chant "Four legs good, two legs better"?

   A. Napoleon
   B. Moses
   C. Clover
   D. Squealer

6.   What is Sugarcandy Mountain?

    A.   The name of the lullaby that Napoleon forces the pigeons to sing to his thirty-one piglets

    B.   The idea of animal heaven propagated by Moses the raven

    C.   The setting for the story that Mollie tells to the lambs

    D.   The mountain visible on Animal Farm's horizon

7.   How many letters is Boxer able to learn?

    A.   Four—A through D

    B.   Zero

    C.   Six—the number of different letters in Napoleon's name

    D.   All twenty-six, plus certain letters in the Russian Cyrillic alphabet

8.   Which of the pigs proves the best writer?

    A.   Napoleon

    B.   Squealer

    C.   Snowball

    D.   Curly

9.   Which pig writes the poem lauding Napoleon?

    A.   Squealer

    B.   Snowball

    C.   Minimus

    D.   Napoleon himself

10. What does Napoleon rename Animal Farm in his toast at the end of the novel?

    A.   Napoleon Farm

    B.   Pig Farm

    C.   Freedonia

    D.   The Manor Farm

11. Why does Napoleon believe that he is dying the morning after he drinks the whisky?

    A. Because he feels a bizarre desire to leave Animal Farm

    B. Because he has a miserable hangover

    C. Because he was visited by the vengeful ghost of Snowball during a drunken trance

    D. Because he was visited by the vengeful ghost of Old Major during a drunken trance

12. With whom does Napoleon play cards at the end of the novel?

    A. Mr. Frederick

    B. Mr. Jones

    C. Mr. Wiltshire

    D. Mr. Pilkington

13. What is the name of the quasi-Marxist socialist philosophy advocated by Napoleon and Snowball?

    A. Porcinism

    B. Animalism

    C. Communalism

    D. Fourleggism

14. What are Boxer's maxims?

    A. Snowball is always right" and "For the glory of Animal Farm"

    B. "I will work harder" and "For the glory of Animal Farm"

    C. "I will work harder" and "Napoleon is always right"

    D. "Snowball is always right" and "I will work harder"

15. Which animal voluntarily leaves the farm?

    A. Mollie

    B. Boxer

    C. Squealer

    D. Napoleon

REVIEW & RESOURCES

16. What is Boxer's ultimate fate?

    A. He dies of old age.
    B. The windmill falls on him.
    C. Napoleon sells him to a glue factory.
    D. Mr. Whymper shoots him.

17. What is Mr. Jones's main vice?

    A. Lust
    B. Alcohol
    C. Gambling
    D. Cigars

18. Which of the following pigs composes the song that replaces "Beasts of England"?

    A. Maximus
    B. Minimus
    C. Snowball
    D. Napoleon

19. What title does Napoleon eventually assume for himself?

    A. King of the Animals
    B. Lord of Manor Farm
    C. President of the Republic
    D. God of Beasts

20. Which animal refuses to become excited about the windmill?

    A. Old Major
    B. Old Benjamin
    C. Boxer
    D. Clover

21. What is the reason for the windmill's initial collapse?

    A. Snowball sabotages it.
    B. The farmers blow it up with dynamite.
    C. It falls in a storm.
    D. Napoleon sabotages it and frames Snowball.

22. Which animal discovers the truth about Boxer's destination when the pigs load him into a cart claiming that he is being taken to a doctor?

   A. Mollie
   B. Muriel
   C. Clover
   D. Benjamin

23. Which Russian leader does Snowball most resemble?

   A. Lenin
   B. Trotsky
   C. Stalin
   D. Gorbachev

24. Which Russian leader does Napoleon most resemble?

   A. Stalin
   B. Trotsky
   C. Tsar Nicholas
   D. Khrushchev

25. What Russian institution does the raven Moses evoke?

   A. The Secret Police
   B. The Congress
   C. The Russian Orthodox Church
   D. The education system

ANSWER KEY

1: D; 2: B; 3: C; 4: A; 5: D; 6: B; 7: A; 8: C; 9: C; 10: D; 11: B; 12: D;
13: B; 14: C; 15: A; 16: C; 17: B; 18: B; 19: C; 20: B; 21: C; 22: D;
23: B; 24: A; 25: C

Suggestions for Further Reading

BLOOM, HAROLD, ed. *George Orwell's* ANIMAL FARM. New York: Chelsea House Publishers, 1999.

DAVISON, PETER. *George Orwell: A Literary Life.* New York: St. Martin's Press, 1996.

FOWLER, ROGER. *The Language of George Orwell.* New York: St. Martin's Press, 1996.

GROSS, MIRIAM, ed. *The World of George Orwell.* London: Weidenfeld and Nicolson, 1971.

MARX, KARL. *The Communist Manifesto.* New York: Bantam Books, 1991.

MEYERS, JEFFREY, ed. *George Orwell: The Critical Heritage Series.* London: Routledge, 1997.

O'NEILL, TERRY. *Readings on* ANIMAL FARM. San Diego, CA: Greenhaven Press, 1998.

PIPES, RICHARD, and PETER DIMOCK. *A Concise History of the Russian Revolution.* New York: Alfred A. Knopf, 1996.

WILLIAMS, RAYMOND. *Orwell.* London: Fontana Press, 1991.

REVIEW & RESOURCES